EMERGENCY CALL

From the second room on the left, there came a tremendous groaning. Thank God I had come urgently; there was obviously something really amiss. I tried the door handle. It would not budge. There didn't appear to be anybody else in the house and the door was almost falling off its hinges, so I put my shoulder to it, bursting into the bedroom.

There, instead of the ailing Mrs Sanderson, was one of her daughters. She lay naked in the middle of a large double bed, covered by an equally naked middle-aged man in the middle of something his wife would certainly not have approved of.

'Oh, there you are, doctor. Thank you for calling. Mother felt better so she's gone out to do the shopping.'

There You Are, Doctor!

DR ROBERT CLIFFORD

Illustrated by Larry

SPHERE BOOKS LIMITED

A SPHERE BOOK

First published in Great Britain by Pelham Books Ltd 1986
Published by Sphere Books Ltd 1988
1st reprint 1989
2nd reprint 1990

Printed and bound in Great Britain by
BPCC Hazell Books
Aylesbury, Bucks, England
Member of BPCC Ltd.

ISBN 0 7474 0035 0

Sphere Books Ltd
A Division of
Macdonald & Co (Publishers) Ltd
Orbit House, 1 New Fetter Lane, London EC4A 1AR
A member of Maxwell Macmillan Pergamon Publishing Corporation

For Cliff, Joyce, Clive, Petra, Janet and Sarah

Contents

	Prologue	viii
1	Naked Truth	1
2	Horses for Courses	8
3	Round and About	13
4	A Collection of Characters	19
5	Family Matters	37
6	Clanger Bartlett	53
7	Dimming Lights	59
8	Fishing Lessons	67
9	Tooth for a Tooth	77
10	Unquenchable Thirsts	83
11	Sabbatical Leave	90
12	Auntie Kitty	106
13	Medical Advances	116
14	Creatures Small and Small	121
15	Different Ways	130
16	Going Home	142
	Postscript	150

Prologue

Life is a tragedy, for we are all born eventually to die. We survive our tragedies by laughing at them.

A friend once told me that when he was under the influence of ether he dreamed he was turning over the pages of a great book, in which he knew he would find, on the last page, the meaning of life.

The pages of the book were alternately tragic and comic, and he turned page after page, his excitement growing, not only because he was approaching the answer, but because he couldn't know, until he arrived, on which side of the book the final page would be. At last it came: the universe opened up to him in a hundred words: and they were uproariously funny.

He came back to consciousness crying with laughter, remembering everything. He opened his lips to speak. It was then that the great and comic answer plunged back out of his reach.

Christopher Fry

CHAPTER 1

Naked Truth

An urgent message was waiting for me when I arrived at the surgery; it was another of those ambiguous calls from Mrs Sanderson. No details, but would the doctor come straight-away, please?

Dare I leave it until after my surgery? I had been on so many wild-goose chases to Mrs Sanderson's that it seemed a reasonable risk. The first time she called me out urgently she had a ruptured appendix; another time she had broken a hip; but quite often – at least thirty or forty times – I had been summoned in haste to find that she hadn't even been in, having miraculously recovered and gone out to the launder-ette or somewhere. I decided to wait until after the surgery.

I saw my first patient, who had arrived ten minutes before time. Then Grace, one of our receptionists, rang through to say there was nobody waiting for me. The town must have been smitten by a sudden outbreak of health. 'Oh hell,' I thought, 'let's get this over with.'

I shot over to Mrs Sanderson's. It meant leaving the surgery and crossing the bridge to go up to the uphill part of Tad-chester, then down through a long winding estate to an old Victorian house. The house was completely unkempt, barely furnished and filled with all sorts of lodgers and hangers-on, plus Mrs Sanderson's four daughters. It had been suggested that a red light outside the place would not be amiss.

I banged at the front door. There was no reply. This wasn't unusual. I went round to the back door and shouted – again, no reply, though the back door was unlocked. There were altogether about seven or eight bedrooms in this tumbledown house. I would have to find out which one she was hiding in. I climbed the stairs shouting, 'Hallo—oo! Hallo—oo!' Still no reply.

I looked around the first landing, trying to decide which room to attempt first. The choice was made for me when, from the second room on the left, there came a tremendous groaning. Thank God I had come urgently; there was obviously something really amiss. I tried the door handle. It would not budge. There didn't appear to be anybody else in the house and the door was almost falling off its hinges, so I put my shoulder to it, bursting into the bedroom.

There, instead of the ailing Mrs Sanderson, was one of her not unattractive daughters. She lay naked in the middle of a large double bed, covered by an equally naked middle-aged man in the middle of something his wife certainly would not have approved of. His activities could not have been helped by the door's crashing down beside the bed; a sort of added climax, as it were.

The naked man, stilled by my entrance, lay with his head tucked into the pillow, obviously not wanting to be recognised, but there seemed to be something familiar about the boil on the back of his neck.

Meanwhile Miss Sanderson, smiling sweetly over her companion's rotund shoulder, said, 'Oh, there you are, Doctor. Thank you for calling. Mother felt better so she's gone out to do the shopping.'

With a friendly wave of her hand I was dismissed and so I hurried back to the surgery for my next appointment.

*   *   *

Unnecessary calls, happily, were not too frequent. One of the most irritating came one evening from Tommy Charles, a sort of male Mrs Sanderson, who actually lived only three or four doors away from her. His call came at the end of a long and tiring day. He, like Mrs Sanderson, had presented me now and again with something serious so I couldn't ignore his call. I wearily strode up the path to his old people's bungalow.

'Well, Tommy,' I said, 'what is it this time?'

Tommy was sitting in front of a roaring fire enjoying a mug of tea and a piece of toast.

'I don't feel all that bright, Doctor,' he said. 'But the main thing that's worrying me is all these empty medicine bottles.' He waved towards a box containing about thirty empty bottles, representing several months of his medication, all washed and tidied up in the box.

'Would you mind taking them back to the surgery?' he said. 'I don't like the empties hanging about.'

The fact that we didn't re-use bottles was of no consequence.

3

I didn't feel like upsetting Tommy with a dressing-down, but he never knew how near he came to having the whole box dropped on his head.

During the time I had been in general practice, the amount of home visiting had dwindled from being a major part of the work to a relatively minor one. This wasn't because the nation's health was getting better, but simply because more people had transport of their own or knew somebody who could give them a lift into town. The only time that home visits did pick up was in the summer months when Tadchester Bridge was so crowded with holidaymakers that it often took half an hour to cross it. Some patients felt that they would rather waste the doctor's time than their own, but thankfully they were a very small minority.

As new drug treatments improved, night calls became fewer but were never ignored. It was very rare, if ever, that one was unnecessarily called out after twelve o'clock. Often the only treatment required was the appearance of a doctor who could take responsibility for the situation. I still deemed such calls necessary. Patients who felt they just couldn't cope needed help or reassurance and could have worried themselves to death if they waited until morning for their fears to be allayed.

Also I was not brave enough to refuse to go on these calls. On the odd occasion that I hadn't gone, when it seemed as if some reassurance over the phone might be enough, I had spent a sleepless night wishing I had gone and wondering if I had given them the right advice.

I was the fourth partner in a group of five and a half partners in a little Somerset town called Tadchester. It was a market town with a rising populaton of about eight thousand. It stood on the estuary of the River Tad in one of the most beautiful parts of the Somerset coast, with the resorts of Sanford-on-Sea and Stowin about equidistant east and west of it.

Although primarily a market town, it had in the past centred on its coal mine; there was some fishing, an increasing amount of light industry and a great deal of farming. The town was split in two by the River Tad and further split by the large hill which dominated one side of the river.

You are not just a Tadchester resident, you are strictly Up-the-Hill or Down-the-Hill. In years past this had important social distinctions in that the populations of Up-the-Hill tended to be the have-nots, whereas Down-the-Hill tended to be the haves. They had levelled off over the years with the coming of light industry which was mainly Up-the-Hill. It had encouraged the building of big housing estates, which had created the effect almost of two towns.

There were even two football teams. Tadchester United was the traditional Tadchester football side. It was Down-the-Hill and had a history going back more than 150 years. The team Up-the-Hill called itself Tadchester Royal. This was because at some point way back in the past, a King Charles or Richard or possibly even Henry VIII stayed at an inn on that side of the river. It made the Royals feel they were much superior to poor old Tadchester United, which in some ways they were as they had a better ground and were a better team.

* * *

We were the only general practice in the town and we also took care of the local hospital. Of the five full partners, each had his own area of responsibility in the hospital. Steve Maxwell, the senior partner, had a special interest in medicine. Henry Johnson, the second senior, was the surgeon. Jack Hart, the third partner, was the anaesthetist.

I, as the fourth partner, was reckoned to be the expert of midwifery, although in recent years this meant just pointing the expectant mothers in the direction of the hospital. Midwifery had changed so much that instead of doing three home confinements a fortnight I now was lucky if I did one or two a year, the rest being handled by the big new maternity hospital at Winchcombe.

Our fifth partner was Ron Dickinson, an accomplished athlete who spent a great deal of his time running, jumping, swimming, sailing, water-skiing and removing all the local tonsils.

When I had a coronary bypass operation a couple of years before, we had a locum, Catherine Carlton to cover my work. Catherine, the wife of a local dentist, was kept on as a half-time partner when I returned to duty.

Catherine was a delightful girl who balanced the load by sharing weekend and night duties, and who increased the practice lists by two when she produced twins just a year after she had been made a half-time partner.

In my advancing years, all young doctors look as if they should still be sitting their 'A' levels rather than practising medicine, and Catherine was one of these. Like her husband Tony, who not only practised dentistry but played a vigorous part in the affairs of the town council, both of them had pilots' licences. Whereas my family would think we were adventurous motoring through France, Catherine and Tony would fly to Malta or some other such place, piloting their own machine.

We were a happy and well-balanced team and having a new part-time lady member to add to the five was what we needed to round us off. There are some subjects that ladies only want to talk about to ladies.

We were all very lucky to be practising medicine in such delightful surroundings. Doctors in Tadchester were very important people. They ranked with vicars and solicitors as the leading lights of the town. If someone was to be successful in any other field apart from farming, then he had to go away up to London or to one of the big cities. It gave us an inflated idea of our own importance. Talking to a colleague who was in practice in a large town in Berkshire, I found that doctors there came much further down the batting order. They had to compete with airline pilots, merchant bankers, members of Parliament and property dealers. As my friend said, he often felt that he was just a clerk who had to supply notes before a patient could see a specialist.

We were indeed lucky. We had the championship golf course at Sanford-on-Sea; a flourishing sailing club at Stowin; the River Tad and its companion the River Tod, at Winchcombe, not far away. There was much unspoilt country and, as yet undiscovered by too many of the general public, coves and tiny beaches tucked away in quiet corners. It was a good place both to live and work in.

CHAPTER 2

Horses for Courses

Following the death of the octogenarian vicar of St Peter's Church, Up-the-Hill, the new young vicar had made a disastrous start. At his welcoming party, his heavily built hostess's right breast broke loose from its moorings, and was exposed for all to see. Instead of what I understand is the classical way of repairing the situation — gently returning the object with a warm tablespoon — the bright young man shouted, 'Look out of the window everybody!' Everybody looked out of the window. And there on the lawn were two dogs mating.

It was the beginning of a series of disasters in Tom Leatherbridge's new ministry. Part of this was that any new vicar represented such change: the previous incumbent had held the post for more than sixty years. At his first christening, young Tom dropped the baby in the font and cut its head, leaving it in need of two stitches. This was a first as far as I was concerned.

Tom was a northerner, with a hearty sense of humour and bonhomie not in tune with the rather fixed southern ways of Tadchester. He was a leg-puller, but many of his parishioners didn't understand his humour. Slowly, an area of viciousness and gossip sprang up round him. Three middle-aged ladies in

the Mothers' Union implied that he had made improper suggestions to them. The only thing the three had in common was they would have been a great success at a Hallowe'en ball, even without masks. They were leaders in the behind-the-scenes whispering campaign against this poor young man.

Two choirboys who were obviously avid readers of one of the Sunday newspapers, where there were countless stories of misbehaviour between vicars and choirboys, reported to their parents that he had looked at them in a funny way. Before long this amounted almost to homosexual rape, and the parents withdrew them from the choir.

An atmosphere of hate and viciousness that only a small community can generate grew up round this unfortunate, but most likeable, young man, all stemming from the one unhappy incident at his introduction to the parish. It was almost now as if he bore a coat-of-arms that included a pair of mating dogs. He was progressively shunned by his parishioners as more and more people imagined he had insulted them or done something. He wasn't invited out. His congregation began to fall away and there was even talk of the three harridans having complained to the police of his improper advances. It was beginning to destroy him.

What I knew, but nobody else knew, was that soon after he had arrived he had been steadily and properly courting a sister from the fever hospital. It was she who persuaded him to talk to me about his troubles.

He came to me one evening in utter misery, pouring out all the unjustified troubles that had been heaped upon him.

I listened sympathetically and tried to reassure him. When he asked me what to do I said, and I believed it, that I'd always felt there were horses for courses. The answer was simple: he probably wasn't the right horse for this course.

I said, 'I think your employer,' pointing upwards towards the Almighty, 'really means you to do work elsewhere.'

'Do you really mean that, Doctor?' he said.

'Yes, of course,' I said, breaking one of my rules that I wouldn't behave like a deity myself. 'I think a change of scene is the only answer.'

Tom Leatherbridge was a northern lad used to northern people, brought up in an industrial town.

'You don't think I'm running away?' he said.

'No,' I said, pointing upwards again. 'I think it's Him. He's just trying to show you you ought to be somewhere else.'

Perhaps there was something in Tom that had lain hidden. He had escaped from the hard industrial north to the balmy south; something on his conscience told him he ought to go back to the muck and brass of the north, a move which was now often being suggested by his parishioners.

I appeared to have lifted a tremendous load from him.

'Thank you, Doctor,' he said. 'God bless you.'

He handed in his resignation to his local church council which was readily accepted, served about a month's notice, and easily found a parish near to where he was brought up in the north. A couple of months later his fiancée from the fever hospital went up and married him. Pam and I went up to the wedding and found he was already happily settled in an adoring parish with a packed church, and he had become a most popular young man.

His abrupt departure from Tadchester brought all sorts of more vicious rumours about him: that he had made three girls pregnant, that he had been unfrocked, that he had gone to South Africa, that the BBC had taken him on. I was utterly amazed at the bad feeling people had got for this very innocent, inoffensive, sincere, hard-working young man.

I am not usually vindictive, but when I came back from his wedding I went round to everybody I knew who had been unpleasant or had made half hints about him. The three harridans who were supposed to have been improperly propositioned I interviewed independently with a little notebook at my side, frightening them that police action was going to be taken for slander. The simple answer in their case was that there was nothing more they would have liked than to have been propositioned, but the chances of it were almost nil. Their only hope lay in stumbling across a blindfolded sex-maniac. I roasted the parents and the choirboys who had cast aspersions, and for a few days anybody who had said anything detrimental about Tom Leatherbridge got the sharp end of my tongue. There was, of course, nothing against him. He had been just a round peg in a square hole.

Eventually the community Up-the-Hill became sufficiently ashamed to send him an overgenerous wedding present, with many thanks for all his care of them.

A full time minister was found to replace Tom; an older man, Ross Stone, and his wife Bettine. Ross Stone's first job after ordination many years before, had been as a curate at St Peter's so he and his wife knew the people and the area very well. Ross was the epitome of everything that was good in an Anglican minister or any minister, or in fact any person. He was just a good man. His wife, Bettine, was a handsome and gracious woman, perfect as a vicar's wife, joining in every single activity connected with the female side of the church, all the women's organisations and the children's organisations, many of which must have thoroughly bored her, but whether they did or not she always appeared to enjoy them.

Ross was a true man of God. Whenever I was called out to a death, whether the patient was a churchgoer, Roman Catholic, Jewish or nonconformist, I would usually find Ross there when I arrived or he would arrive as I left. The aged and lonely whom I visited routinely, so did he, and we seemed to follow each other around. He was a kind, caring, comforting man who went about amongst his flock just doing good.

I am afraid that Pam and I were not churchgoers. The only time that we did go to church was usually for funerals or weddings. This did not stop us from becoming good friends with the Stones. We often used to dine at the vicarage and they often came and had a meal with us.

Unfortunately, Ross was approaching retiring age when he arrived back in Tadchester, so was with us in all far too short a time. But we have kept in touch and seen each other from time to time, and they have happily always remained good friends.

St Peter's was at its best under Ross. He cut out the cant and hypocrisy and his influence of good spread amongst the parishioners. It's amazing how a community can make about-turns so quickly. I think my day of spitefulness had helped Ross, for the three harridans, the choirboys and their families, and one or two others, never appeared at the church again. It was some dead wood well cut out. Some had become Methodists and some Baptists, so they obviously couldn't do without a church of some sort. I hoped they hadn't taken their ability to poison the atmosphere with them.

CHAPTER 3

Round and About

Whenever the rare occasion of a sunny day and time off coincided, my wife Pam and I would slip away and drive to Green Cliff. We knew of a secret path that led to a little ledge that gave a panoramic view of the whole area of coast.

Most days, particularly if the sun was going to be followed by rain, Puffin Island, twenty miles off the coast of Sanford-on-Sea, stood out etched on the horizon. In years gone by it was a pirate stronghold, but it was now owned by the National Trust with a dozen residents, rare species of plants and assorted animals, including peacocks, and a herd of wild goats that destroyed everything in front of them. Two-and-a-half miles long and half-a-mile wide, the island was a natural paradise. There was one hotel and a dozen cottages that were let out in the summer.

If we were lucky we would see, like dots, the crowds on the beach at Sandimere, the great pebble ridge sweeping in an arc over several miles right to the mouth of the Tad, the drab-looking huts of the holiday camps, a couple of fishing boats trawling and a paddle steamer taking day-trippers from Coomten, a port twenty miles west of Winchcombe to Puffin Island. The trippers would struggle up from the island's rocky

landing stage just in time to buy some souvenirs before they came back.

To the south we could see Hovery, the most picturesque village in the area, like a cleft in the rocks, with steep cobbled streets that went down and down and down. Goods were transported by donkey and sledge, and every year three or four holiday-makers had coronaries after climbing down just a bit farther than they meant to.

We could see from our vantage point small sailing dinghies from the Stowin Yacht Club, a few pleasure boats bobbing up and down with fishing parties on board, a coastal vessel making for Tadchester and the regular supply ship, a small forty-five-foot trawler, the *Puffin*, carrying the essentials out to Puffin Island and often a dozen holiday-makers as well.

Peargate with its shipyard stood out clearly, and even from several miles away the clanging noises of shipbuilding could be heard. The Peargate lifeboat lay patiently moored out in the sea on the sea side of the sand bar, ready whatever the state of the tide to dash off to a rescue.

I don't think there was anywhere that provided a more picturesque scene than this, providing the sun shone. Alas, we had one of the heaviest rainfalls in the country. If we were caught in our vantage spot by an unpredicted rain shower, not only did it spoil the view, we would get soaking wet in the two-mile scramble downhill to reach our car.

It is amazing what changes had taken place since the Industrial Revolution. Only a hundred years ago it took a day to travel from Hovery to Tadchester, so people didn't often do it. They lived in self-contained little communities in every access to the beach all the way round the bay. What in those days used to be a whole day's journey, with probably a few highwaymen to be negotiated, was now covered by twenty-five minutes in the car.

Tadchester had not been too spoilt by modern developments. Many of the buildings dated back to the 16th century, and the place engendered a feeling of safety and stability. Most of the buildings were white, and there was even a town song about the little white town by the sea.

* * *

One of the most attractive features of Tadchester was that it was one of the cleanest ports that I have ever seen, one of the few that had no accompanying railway. All that came into Tadchester was two or three regular fishing boats and a few timber boats from Scandinavia, an occasional collier, gravel dredgers from the Channel, then boats with loads such as concrete and occasionally flour. There was usually one boat moored on Tadchester quay, very rarely two, and I think that the maximum in tonnage that they could take that far up the river was 2,000 tons.

We were about three-and-a-half miles upstream from where the Tad and the River Tod, coming from Winchcombe, joined. Stowin was at the middle of the confluence of these two

rivers and on the Tadchester side was the shipbuilding area of Peargate.

Most of Tadchester's spotless quay was an auxiliary car park. About once every two years a visitor would put his foot on the accelerator rather than the brake and we would have a tragedy, whether the tide was in or out.

There were few more picturesque sights on a sunny day with the tide going out, than to see the licensed seine-net fishermen with their nets fishing from the bridge pools. I could watch them for hours, fascinated, but it was when the tide was in that Tadchester looked at its best.

I remember one day at a wedding on the Up-the-Hill side of the water at a hotel near Stowin, seeing a couple of fishing boats coming up the river, bathed in glorious sunshine. A little

16

coaster having unloaded its cargo on to Tadchester's neat quay, was moving downriver. A couple of rowing fours from the Tadchester rowing clubs, the Reds and the Blues, were making even time with a couple of sailing boats. It was all peace and tranquillity.

The clean, peaceful, unindustrialised quay changed suddenly, literally almost overnight, into a filthy place with queues of lorries, snarled-up traffic and boats queuing up to come into the berths. The reason for this was the coal strike of 1984. Tadchester was an unlicensed port and was a loophole by which coal could get into the country. There never seemed to be any pickets down there trying to stop it.

From a leisurely timber boat once a fortnight, we had four or five coal boats from all over the place unloading on to the quay, with coal dust and grit sweeping all over the main quay road. A stream of lorries stretched back as far as the huge new Western Counties offices at the end of the quay. There was Polish coal, Australian coal, American coal, Chinese coal, Russian coal, Rumanian coal. I used to have a good look at it, as just before going up to medical school I had had two years in the mines as a Bevin Boy and reckoned I was an authority on coal. My coal was the rich, gleaming Barnsley bed from South Yorkshire. The stuff I saw coming in was a mixture of slate and coal dust and this was how it seemed to burn.

It went on for months and months. I forget the precise figures of the coal import into Tadchester but it went from something like six thousand tons in one year to 760,000 tons. A good 700 tons of that seemed to get into my eye every time I walked along the quay. It completely changed the town for a while. Every man who could drive a lorry had a job. The unloading went on day and night and seemed to go on for ever. We wondered when eventually the strike finished whether things would ever return to normal.

A lot of money was spent by foreign ships' crews and lorry drivers, so one man's loss was another man's fortune. For a time Tadchester thrived, but it was losing its character. The miners' strike eventually came to an end, but we wondered if the coal would still keep coming. Perhaps somebody had found that this was cheaper than buying coal produced in England. The boats kept coming in numbers for two weeks after the strike then they started to dwindle; finally they disappeared altogether. It was a further three months before the stains and coal dust were washed away by a combination of winter snow and rain and the municipal street sweepers. But, come the spring, the quay was restored to its old beauty again.

It did show how nothing is settled, how quickly in this moving world things that seemed permanent can change. It seemed mean in a way to grumble; we hadn't been inconvenienced a lot, we hadn't gone short of fuel. A lot of people had found employment, though at somebody else's expense. But the big grumble was that our sleepy, beautiful little town had for a few long months been turned into a grimy industrial suburb.

A year later, a new bridge was begun over the Tad, of a structure which meant that none of the coastal vessels would be able to pass above it to the quay. Until the bridge was finished, we wouldn't know whether it would enhance the town or be an eyesore, though one thing was sure: it would protect us from ever becoming a hectic industrial port again.

Selfish? Perhaps. But the world holds plenty of dirt and squalor. It doesn't hold too many places like Tadchester.

CHAPTER 4

A Collection of Characters

I'm sure that every general practice feels that it has more than its share of eccentrics. I know that we in Tadchester did. We perhaps had some grounds for this as the town had plenty of out-of-the-way places where people could almost disappear from public view. But if perhaps we over-estimated the quantity of our eccentric patients, certainly they didn't lack in quality.

One of our prizewinners was Hamish Richardson. His eccentricity was such that we didn't learn much about him until after he died. He came to Tadchester before I arrived – a well-educated man with a little money of his own – and proceeded to build himself a stockade in a copse near Elfin Cross. He had the absolute minimum of contact with the outside world and was almost completely self-sufficient. He had an arrangement with a local farmer that if he was ever in distress or needed help, he would fly a white flag from the tall flagpole sticking out from the middle of his stockade.

One day I was summoned by the farmer. Would I go and see Hamish Richardson?

'It'll be quite safe,' he said.

I didn't quite know what he meant but I got there, having

driven up to Elfin Cross, then driven two miles along a muddy lane, then walked a further mile to a wooden stockade straight out of *Treasure Island*.

The stockade consisted of an area of about a hundred yards long by thirty-five yards wide surrounded by tree trunks, sharpened at the top and standing twelve feet high. In the middle of this area was a log cabin and nearby was a wire cage with two bull mastiffs trying to tear their way out. Normally, apparently, they were left to roam at will. The one incongruous thing about the whole back-to-nature atmosphere, was two large Calor gas cylinders behind the cabin.

As I walked to the cabin, I took a quick look round. There were hens scuttling around inside the stockade, there were pigs grunting in one corner, and a goat very much in milk tethered to one side. There was a well with a shiny bucket attached to a rope and outside the gate at the back of the stockade was about half an acre of immaculately-kept garden, jammed full of every possible vegetable.

I had been asked by the farmer to bring some cough medicine and antibiotics; Mr Richardson had a chest infection.

I entered the log cabin. It was plain but comfortable and everything was neat and tidy. There were wooden tables, a rocking chair, a wood-burning stove, Calor gas stove, a couple of Calor gas lights and some oil lamps. There was no radio, no television, and just one row of books, all about gardening and growing things.

Mr Richardson was in the next room, a quiet, neatly-kept bedroom, in a sleeping bag on a bunk. He had an obviously bad chest, and asked me politely if I had brought him some antibiotics and cough medicine.

'Yes,' I said.

'Thank you very much, Doctor,' he said. 'I'll let you know if I require you again. Don't ever try and come here without being sent for. The dogs could tear you to bits.'

I could quite believe that.

Back in Tadchester, I enquired about Mr Richardson's background. Nobody was very forthcoming. He was about as self-sufficient as any man could be. Joe and Lynne Church had a nodding acquaintance with him. He was a keen fisherman, lobster catcher and prawner, and they would bump into him as he combed the beaches each day, travelling there by an old bike with a huge basket on the back. He had a map of all the lobster holes in the coves in the area, and usually made a good haul of lobsters, which he sold to hotels in the town. He appeared in the town once a week on Fridays at the local pannier market, just off the High Street.

Every Friday he sat behind a table piled with the very best vegetables, free range eggs, the odd chicken, goat's cheese, and occasionally such delicacies as smoked trout. His was always the first stall to make for, as the quality of all his goods was so much better than anybody else's. He was quiet and personable, did not communicate with his fellow stallholders but again was not rude. He never got into personal conversation, just brought his goods, set them up, and sold them.

I doubt if he sold enough to cover his expenses, or to make a proper living out of it but, as he just about fed himself completely, perhaps he did.

When the pannier market closed, he would go round the town making a few essential purchases like flour and salt, go into the hardwear shop for nails, screws and odd implements, then back to his stockade. The only other time that you were likely to see him was if he was nipping off on one of his fishing expeditions. There was no report ever of his shooting rabbits or birds, but that is not to say that he didn't; there was always somebody, usually poachers, banging off at something in Elfin Cross.

I was only called to see him once more and that was about ten years after the first visit. He had an infection of one leg which I had to open and dress. I gave him an antibiotic and was able to question him a little about his life and about how he fed himself. There was no doubt he had an adequate and balanced diet. There was a brine barrel in the corner with joints of pork and goat in salt. He had his own smoking room and there were rows of smoked brown trout and sea trout hanging from the

wall. When I started to ask about his past or where he had come from, he clammed up and dismissed me saying, 'Thank you very much. That'll be all for today, Doctor. I'll let you know if I want you again.'

He never ever did send for me again. And he never put up his white flag again.

One severe winter, his farmer contact became suspicious that he hadn't seen anybody around for some time and contacted the police. The bull mastiffs were loose, so nobody dared to go in, but both dogs looked emaciated – and there wasn't a sign of another living thing, pig, goat or chicken. It would appear that the mastiffs had eaten the lot.

A vet was called, who threw some drugged meat to the dogs, who wolfed it up straightaway. Within an hour they were sound asleep and I was with the police when they broke through. First the vet dragged the dogs into the wire cage and then we went into the house to find Hamish Richardson very, very cold and very, very dead in bed. He was frozen stiff and had probably been dead for weeks. The post mortem revealed that he had died from natural causes and only after his death did we learn the details of his life.

He had been a university professor with an MSc and a PhD. He had a brother and a sister in Scotland and apparently his university work had been in some midland university. He had suddenly walked out one day with no explanation, and now it was so long ago there weren't too many people about who remembered him at all.

As far as I could gather, he had lived in his stockade for probably forty years, and was round about his eighties when he died. He had lived completely alone, apart from his animals, and it would appear was quite happy. He never interfered with anybody and he made sure that nobody interfered with him.

I often wondered what started it all. Was it a scandal? Some broken love affair? We would never know. All we knew was that a distinguished man of learning had suddenly thrown it all up to go and live the life, the very lonely life, of a primitive backwoodsman.

He had done this successfully and I could not help but admire him. He really could not be classified as a true eccentric: he was just different. He must have been a man of tremendous inner strength and self-sufficiency to cope single-handed and create his own domain. I knew that I would never have wanted to live like that, even if I could have coped.

His life and lonely death moved me in a way I couldn't explain. There was something rather fine about it all. I went to his funeral, to which none of his family came. Any survivors were too old, too far away and too out of touch to make it. When the vicar said, 'God rest his soul,' I felt myself echoing those words.

*   *   *

Zackovitch Hebden lived in two caravans in a small copse of trees about fifty yards from the walls of a small brickmaking plant on the outskirts of Tadchester. He was not a Romany. We had our own Romanies – they were much too respectable to be called Gypsies – who lived in five settled caravans on the other side of Tadchester. These caravans were immaculate, very expensive, had every mod con, were filled with precious china and the owners were as nice a group of people as one could wish to meet anywhere.

I looked after only one member of this group, a Miss Rowley. She explained that although they were settled, two or three times a year they felt the urge to be on the move, and would go off and join some travelling Romanies.

'It's in the blood, Doctor,' she said. 'The year is never the same unless I do some travelling.'

Zackovitch Hebden never travelled anywhere. He never left Tadchester and its precincts. His two caravans were broken down, derelict, with no electricity, water or sanitation. His wife – who was almost crippled with arthritis – had to walk across a field with a milk churn to get the water from a stand pipe. What they did about sanitation, I never enquired. I just noticed that the grass in the area of the caravans looked rather richer than the grass beyond them.

Zackovitch – who was always Zackovitch, nobody would ever think of calling him Zack – lived in a daytime caravan which was equipped with Calor gas and where his meals were cooked by his long-suffering wife. At night he slept in the other caravan which was warmed by a smelly paraffin stove. He made up for any lack of heating by wearing layers and layers of grubby clothes. I was continually urging him to go into housing and the social services offered him council flats and council houses. Though his wife was keen, he always refused. He wasn't short of money and always ran a good car, new enough to have cost him a fair amount.

I never knew the derivation of Zackovitch's name. He was in actual fact a Yorkshireman, from where in Yorkshire I don't know, unless it was Hebden Bridge. He was of indeterminate age: he could have been old enough to have served in the First World War or he could have been a First World War baby. There was a rumour during the First World War that the Russians were passing through England because somebody had seen them at a railway station up north with snow on their boots. Perhaps Zackovitch's mother had happened to be in the station waiting room at the time.

Why he chose to live in such discomfort, nobody knew. In winter it used to be appalling. I treated him for pneumonia and had to go through eight or nine layers of clothes to reach his chest. But he recovered, refusing all along to go to hospital.

One Monday I came back from a weekend off to find an urgent call from him – he would never see any doctor but me. He had been having a little waterworks trouble for some time and hadn't passed any water since the Friday night. Finding that I wasn't on duty he was determined to wait until I came back.

I went early and found him in considerable pain with a stomach so swollen that he looked pregnant. There was a tremendous argument about whether he should go into hospi-

tal or not. I refused to try and catheterise him on the spot and told him he would probably need an operation. In the end he reluctantly agreed to go to hospital. A catheter was inserted and he was back in his caravan that night.

'No more hospitals for me,' he said. 'Once is enough.'

At the time Zackovitch had his trouble, catheters were not as sophisticated as they are today. They were made of a substance that meant they would eventually block off, and had to be changed at least once a month, sometimes more. I spent a lot of time in the most unhygienic surroundings, particularly in mid-winter, inserting new catheters into Zackovitch in the most difficult circumstances, with only the relevant piece of anatomy on display, surrounded by a mass of grubby clothing.

I had a patient when I first went into practice who became an expert at catheterising himself, keeping a catheter wrapped in newspaper in his hat. He never washed it, just fished it out and inserted it whenever he felt his tank was full. Zackovitch couldn't take his own catheter out; by this time they had progressed to the extent that they were kept in the bladder by a little balloon. The balloon was filled with water through a tube that ran alongside the catheter and would blow up to the size of a small tangerine.

One weekend the catheter became clogged. Zackovitch rang up to enquire whether I was on duty and being told 'No' he said, 'Never mind'. Henry who was on duty for the weekend, rang to tell me of the call, so I thought I had better look in at the caravans.

I found Zackovitch quite happily wandering round the copse.

'How are things?' I said. 'I've come to change your catheter.'

'No need doctor,' he said. 'I pulled it out myself.'

The very thought of him pulling it out with this tangerine–sized bag attached to the end, made me wince.

'I'm not having one of those things in again,' he said. 'No need. I've passed water fine ever since.'

Zackovitch had done the equivalent of a man efficiently cleaning a rifle barrel. How on earth he had done it I don't know but his good pull-through seemed to work. From then on he had no further trouble with his waterworks.

I never knew much about him, nor could I find out even how he had landed up in these two caravans. His wife, a simple soul, was so concerned with her own troubles (she was getting progressively crippled with arthritis), that she was not much help either.

I had got quite fond of Zackovitch in a way and certainly admired his courage, and a doctor is always flattered when a patient will only see him and nobody else. But after his pull-through, he bothered me less and less. I would occasionally see him and his wife in the town, shopping. I was called once more to the caravans, this time to see Mrs Hebden who had sprained an ankle carrying the water across the field. Again I pleaded with Zackovitch to find better accommodation, but he wouldn't hear of it.

After my coronary bypass operation I was off work for six months. When I came back I started to pick up the threads and contact my old patients. One day I popped in to see Zackovitch and his wife. They were gone. The dilapidated caravans were empty and had been vandalised; windows were smashed, doors torn off and scanty bits of furniture thrown all over the place. There was no record of Zackovitch going into any housing accommodation locally and as far as I knew he had no family. That was the last I thought that I would hear or see of them.

A year later Steve Maxwell was driving up north to see some relative near Birmingham. Turning off the motorway just south of Birmingham he spotted two dilapidated caravans in the cutting underneath the motorway. There was a crippled old lady struggling with a milk churn towards the caravans and a man wrapped in grubby clothing sitting at the caravan door, impatiently waiting. 'I could have sworn they were the Hebdens,' said Steve, 'but there was no way I could pull off the road.'

I'm afraid I wasn't prepared to get my car out and shoot up to Birmingham just to see if it was Zackovitch, so I never knew what became of him.

*   *   *

Miss Peabody worked at the income tax office on Tadchester Quay. She was the sort of person who could not be called anything other than Miss Peabody, nor work anywhere other than in an income tax office.

She was short, plump, grey haired, wore glasses and was completely ageless. At a guess I would have said she was seventy-five but, knowing that she was a civil servant with a retiring age of sixty, I realised she must be less than that unless she had special dispensation.

She was such a permanent fixture at the local income tax office that I had visions of the cleaning ladies dusting her as part of their duties.

She was much like one of our venerable bishops whom I saw when watching a royal wedding at Eric's Radio and TV shop one day. Seeing this snowy-haired, round-shouldered old man tottering up the aisle with only his shepherd's crook keeping him from falling on his face, I said, 'There's a grand old man.'

'Do you know how old he is?' said Eric.

'No,' I said, 'but I should think he's creeping up towards the Queen's telegram.'

'In fact,' said Eric, 'he's only forty-five. He's been practising being eighty ever since he's been forty.'

Miss Peabody was of this ilk. She lived in a neat council flat in the centre of the town. But she had an ambition.

If you asked her what she was going to do in the future she said, quite assuredly, 'I'm going to win the football pools. When I've won them I shall buy a villa in Spain, and when I retire I shall go and live in Spain in the sunshine.'

Although everybody else that I'd ever met was sure that one day they were going to win the pools, I never met anybody quite like Miss Peabody who was absolutely, positively certain she was going to win. It was as if she had had some divine message.

On her annual holiday to Hastings each year, Miss Peabody made several day trips to Calais and Boulogne, so she had already acquired a taste for Continental life.

The win didn't come in a hurry as she filled her pools in, week after week, year after year, on a very modest stake. But Miss Peabody pressed confidently on.

She was very rarely ill, but one Monday morning, she came to the surgery, grey-faced and tight-lipped, and asked for two tranquillisers.

It was taking every bit of her self-control to hold herself together, but she would give no reason.

'Could I just have two tranquillisers doctor? Just the two tablets. I don't mind how much it costs.'

It was the sort of request I got from people who were taking their driving tests for the tenth time and wanted something to steady their nerves the night before. I acceded to her request, wondering what emotional traumas had induced this state in this most staid little lady. Perhaps it was a love affair. No. On second thoughts . . .

I learnt two days later that Miss Peabody, as she had always said she would, had won the football pools. She hadn't won a giant amount, just £20,000. True to her word, she spent £15,000 of it on buying an apartment in southern Spain. To my amazement I found that she was only fifty-five and she was going to use the apartment for holidays until she reached her retiring age of sixty, when she would go to live there. It was nice having the extra £5,000 for furnishing and incidental expenses.

Miss Peabody went off and had three weeks in Spain, thoroughly enjoying it and getting to know the people. It should have been the end of a happy story.

But, alas, when she went back next spring for an early holiday, she found her apartment had been vandalised. The electricity had been cut off and there were all sorts of complex Spanish regulations to deal with. It was all more than she could cope with. She put the flat up for sale. She lost a bit of money on it, not too much, but her dream of living in the sunshine in Spain disappeared.

With the money she salvaged, she bought a nice little house near the park in Tadchester, quiet and away from the noisy council block she lived in. So her winning had been a great bonus, even if her main objective hadn't been achieved. She duly worked on until her retirement, then spent the time in her own house with its nice little garden. She had her library books, belonged to several women's organisations and was a strict churchgoer, so time didn't hang heavily on her hands.

She had bronchitis a couple of winters after she had retired. I popped in to see her. She was lying, covered in blankets, on a chaise longue in her dining room. Covering the dining room table was a mass of football pool forms from about every pools firm in the land. Having checked her over, I asked about her pools. Was she having another go?

'Yes, Doctor,' she replied. 'I'm quite certain that I'm going to win the pools again but this time I think I might look for an apartment in France. I think they're rather more civilised than the Spanish.'

I prescribed for her condition, wished her luck and left her. I thought the chances of her having a second win on the pools were absolutely minute. But for her it was an objective; it might happen any week. If it never happened at all, which was the most likely, she was doing that most important thing, travelling hopefully – which by definition, is supposed to be better than arriving.

*   *   *

Problems that arose in the practice were not just confined to the patients. Not infrequently they involved the partners and their families as well. I remember once coming to the surgery, being handed the phone and told, 'Just listen to this.' There was a child screaming at the top of its voice. When I spoke to the mother I found it was Pam, and it was Paul, one of my own children, who had scalded his hand.

Jack Hart had decided to bring his parents to Tadchester so he could keep a better eye on them. Jack was a gentle, reserved man who was easy to underestimate. It was very difficult to get him to talk about his wartime experiences but he was a doctor working in Hull when the war broke out. He volunteered for the airborne forces, landed in a glider in France soon after D-Day and landed again in a glider during the Rhine crossing. In his second landing the glider came down smack in front of a German machine gun, leaving the troops no alternative but to surrender. Jack spent the rest of the war behind barbed wire in a German prisoner-of-war camp.

During the war Jack's father had served in the Forces as a surgeon, mainly in Africa and sub-tropical areas. Not only did he have to battle for the health of his patients but also spend a tremendous amount of his time and energy on the hygiene of the medical station and the instruments, reducing the chances of cross-infection by making sure that they were sterile and didn't go rusty in the humid surroundings.

Jack's father was a bit eccentric and his mother an absolute dear: one of those little old ladies who was always smiling and who looked as though she were made of porcelain. She was handicapped with arthritis and her husband had to do most of the household shopping and, indeed, most of the housework.

31

In his later years, his eccentricities became more noticeable, probably a reversion to his army surgical days in the jungle. Obsessed about things not being clean and going rusty, he was one of the few people who could empty the whole of a house hot-water system simply by doing the washing-up for two people. Every single item had to be washed thoroughly under a running tap. It had to be dried and then had to be blow-dried with a specially powerful drier. He gave the silver teapot an extra boost on his heater and eventually managed to melt it.

His eccentricities were all quite harmless but they did mean that a great deal of his day was occupied in the simple act of washing a few pots, pans, knives and forks (but alas no more his silver teapot) for two people.

Dr Hart senior had one other idiosyncrasy: his bed. He always refused to buy a new one. The middle of the bed had sunk so much that although his feet and head were at the same level, the rest of his body was down in a deep pit. It was the sort of bed that a camel would have been very happy in, providing it could stick its four feet up in the air. There was a theory that his dipping bed felt like a hammock and reinforced his feeling of being back in the jungle.

He had to go to hospital for a few days and, as Jack's mother couldn't manage on her own, his mother-in-law volunteered to come and hold the fort. There was a difficulty in that there were only two bedrooms in the flat; one occupied by Mrs Hart senior and the other by the bed with the bump in it in old Dr Hart's room. A new bed was ordered to coincide with the day that he was to be admitted to hospital so that it would be a *fait accompli* by the time he came back.

When the time came for him to go to hospital, he decided that he wanted Jack to cut his hair – not that Jack had ever done it before. There was no arguing with his father, so they went into the kitchen and Jack started chopping off a few of his grey locks. In the midst of this the new bed arrived. There was then a sort of French farce, Jack trying to keep his father pinned in the kitchen while the bed was hidden in his wife's bedroom until they eventually got him out of the house.

His stay in hospital wasn't long, but long enough to get him used to a flat bed. He came home and made no comment about the new bed; he seemed to assume that it had always been there. But as soon as he got home, even before he got his coat off, he washed all the cups, plates, knives, saucers, spoons, and anything else he could lay his hands on, carefully drying them, before extensively blow-drying them, including the inside of the new china teapot.

Then he said, 'Thank God. For the first time for days I'll be able to have a clean cup of tea.'

* * *

William Jessop lived in a row of Edwardian houses in a road near the hospital which, in Edwardian times, must have housed the *crème de la crème* of Tadchester society. Many of the houses had been subdivided, some turned into flats, but William Jessop's house was in no way touched; on entering the house you felt you were back in the Edwardian age. It was still filled with the Edwardian furniture of his parents and William

33

himself was an Edwardian figure with a wing collar and a silk cravat with a large diamond pin stuck in the middle of it.

He was an incredible man who knew more about everything than anybody else I've known. He shared his house with a housekeeper-companion, a Miss Winmaker, who was a sort of mental playmate. She could have been a physical playmate too, but somehow I don't think she was, and they were both staunch supporters of the Methodist chapel.

To my knowledge William never went out to work. He played around with stocks and shares and was obviously not short of money. He had a tremendous appetite for knowledge of every kind. He read, and he loved Miss Winmaker to read to him. He played the piano and the organ and was a great authority on music. He was a ham radio operator and conversed with people all over the world. He could speak several languages fluently. And he seemed to know everything about everything.

One day when I had called to see Miss Winmaker, he came down and stopped me.

'Do you know how the distance a furlong developed?' he said.

'No,' I said, thinking about my next case and not wanting to get into a long intellectual discussion with William.

'Well,' he said, 'it was one of the first distances of measurement. What happened was that they got some oxen and they hitched them to a plough and they made a note of how much they could plough in a certain period of time. From then on, that length was called a furlong.'

'Thank you very much, William,' I said, shoving the information into my own memory bank. Perhaps I could get the garage to change the speedometer in my car from miles to furlongs.

William loved to travel.

'So many people think it's the sights of places that are exciting but, to me it's the smells,' he said. 'I love the smell of a place.'

He wrote three philosophical books: when I say wrote, he

34

always used a typewriter, nothing handwritten, and he could type away as fast as the best shorthand typist.

I first met him when he was in his middle sixties and all the time I knew him, he was as busy as a bee. No moment of the day was wasted. If he sent for me it was usually to query me about some new medical advance. He always knew far more about it than I did. He was a very nice man, if a little brusque in manner, and tremendously perceptive. I only had to walk into the room on a visit and he would say, 'What's bothering you today, Dr Clifford?' or 'You seem pleased with yourself today, Dr Clifford,' before I had even opened my mouth, and he was always right. He seemed to have an extra sense about people.

He had some wealthy gentlemen-farmer friends with whom he toured the Continent, Miss Winmaker always making up the party. One of the farmers told me that one day they were driving through Paris and were suddenly lost. They were aiming for Le Touquet.

'I don't know which way to turn,' said the farmer.

'Can you see Notre Dame?' asked William.

'Just,' said the farmer.

'Can you see its shadow?'

'Just,' said the farmer. 'It's pointing to the right.'

'Well, it's twelve o'clock now,' said William, 'take the next turning left and we should be on the road to Le Touquet.'

The farmer did and William was right.

Unfortunately I could never make a friend of William. Not that he was unfriendly, he just lacked the warmth of the old philosophical bookseller at Sanford-on-Sea, Bob Barker, with whom I had many chats. William was really far too intellectual to be chummy.

I would wager an even bet if you asked him any question, be it political, historical, geographical, he would know the answer. He was right up-to-date with current affairs. He always knew who would win an election and by how much. The only thing he wasn't so good on was the weather.

William was quite a remarkable man. In fact, when I look back, probably one of the most remarkable, knowledgeable men I have ever met. The most remarkable thing about him was that you honestly couldn't call him blind, in spite of the fact that at the age of eleven he had completely lost the sight of both eyes.

CHAPTER 5

Family Matters

Pam first started complaining about pains in her hip ten or eleven years back: a bit of stiffness, a bit of pain getting out of bed in the morning. I took notice because Pam was probably the least complaining person I ever knew. (Putting up with me for all these years should confirm that.)

Initially a couple of aspirin put everything all right. There would be no problem for two or three months, then her pain would return, calling for a few more aspirins. During the winter months she had more persistent pain and I or one of my partners would put her on one of the anti-inflammatory drugs that ease joint pain. Oiling the joints, I call it. The drugs relieve pain by taking the inflammation away. By removing inflammation they remove the local pain, as opposed to a pure pain-reliever which relieves any sort of pain. One of the anti-inflammatory drugs would help a little bit with toothache, but not as much as a straightforward pain-killer.

Pam was always better in the summer, and better still if we had been on the Thames with Joe and Lynne. I deduced, thinking man that I am, that having her leaping up lock sides with a rope between her teeth and pulling the boat in was doing her hip good. Anyway, I resolved that from her health point of view, it was much better if I did the steering and she did all the leaping about. She didn't mind this and was actually sure that it kept her pain-free and stopped her being stiff. I encouraged her in this activity and became one of the best steerers on the river.

Pam, Paul, Jane and I once took a canal boat on the Brecon-Abergavenny Canal, a unique canal running parallel to the River Usk, surrounded by villages that seemed to be thirty years back in price as well as time and customs. Paul even caught a trout in the canal and was so confused to find such a beautiful game fish that he unhooked it and put it back in, as he would any coarse fish.

It was a complicated canal full of locks, and Pam had to run across the planks (I haven't a very good head for heights), perch right over the tall locks, and tug on ropes while I hung on grimly to the steering wheel. It was one of the best years her hip ever had. I did think at one time of prescribing boating, or at least land-crewing for patients with painful hips.

However, her hip steadily worsened. She had spells when she was in a good deal of pain. We both accepted the fact that one day we would have to do something about it, but Pam hoped that day was many, many years off.

Her mother, who had been a most courageous lady, had both hips operated on years before artificial hips were thought of. In those days it meant going into hospital for a minimum of twelve weeks in traction, having one hip operated on and then going back six months later for a further twelve weeks while the other hip was done. The operation didn't leave the patient walking about as if nothing had happened, as modern hip operations do. It meant the patient could get about and was relatively pain-free, but that was all.

We gradually went on to stronger and stronger anti-inflammatory preparations. At last Pam agreed to have an X-ray of her hip, and it did show gross arthritic changes. Although by now the anti-inflammatory drugs had begun to upset Pam's stomach a bit, she still wasn't keen on an operation. She had the brilliant idea of joining the over-fifties

38

badminton club; the activity was almost like leaping from a boat. She went to the club twice and thoroughly enjoyed herself, but each time she came back with progressive pain and from then on her hip was sheer agony.

'My love,' I said, 'we've no alternative. We must seek advice.'

There was an orthopaedic surgeon in Winchcombe, Pat Chesterfield, whom I'd known since our student days. 'Let's see him,' I said.

There seemed to be a lot of obstacles.

'I can't have it done before Christmas,' said Pam, 'and then there's Trevor's birthday.'

'Never mind darling,' I said. 'Let's just go and see Pat.'

Pam had a further X-ray which showed that over a period of three months the condition of her hip, almost certainly aggravated by the badminton, had deteriorated markedly. The head of main bone in the leg, the femur, had almost disintegrated.

'You must get this hip done as soon as possible,' said Pat Chesterfield when he saw the X-rays. 'I don't know how you've managed to walk on it.'

Pam went over to Winchcombe to be operated on, coincidentally a year to the day that I had had my coronary bypass operation. She was to have a total hip replacement which would mean removing the whole of the diseased joint and putting in a new artificial one. She felt pretty rough the first day after the operation and was in some pain. The second day she was sitting up taking notice, eating and reading a paper. The third day she was swinging her legs out of bed, thoroughly enjoying being waited on. By the fifth day she was beginning to walk. By the sixth day she was doing some stairs. By the twelfth day she was home, determined not to use sticks, and climbing the stairs unaided.

Within a few weeks she was driving the car and walking into town. Nobody would believe that she had ever had anything wrong with her hip.

We both had our operations on November 23rd. For both of us our first major social event was a New Year's Eve dinner with friends, a sort of first-footing.

Pam was a different woman with her new hip. She was pain-free. She could turn over in bed without any trouble. She was off all drugs. It really was a miracle. We were so fortunate to be born in an age when these great advances in surgery had been made. I certainly, without my operation, would have had to give up work. If there hadn't been these marvellous new artificial hips Pam would have had to undergo the same traumatic experience as her mother and would have finished up, not fully mobile but just pain-free and able to get about only moderately well.

At the time Pam was in hospital there was somebody else having an artificial shoulder put in and somebody else having an artificial knee put in.

Jack Kitchen, an old friend, used to call in and see us with his French wife, Pierette. Now a consultant orthopaedic surgeon at Bath, Jack was the British, if not the world, authority on ankle replacements. He was a huge, broad shouldered, gentle giant who played in the front row with me in my medical student days.

The rugby team called him Garth, after a cartoon character in the *Daily Mirror*, who was a cross between Tarzan and the

Incredible Hulk. Jack was rarely ever roused, but on the rare occasions that the opposing pack did rile him enough to lose his cool, he would seem to swell up about twice his size and sling the opposing set of forwards all over the field.

He had met his wife on a French rugby tour when we were playing in Bordeaux. They always said I had introduced them. I never quite worked out how this had happened but anyway, thirty years later, they were still very happily married. Whenever we met, Jack and I used to have a semi-scrum down to remind us of old times.

As well as being an orthopaedic surgeon, he had written several books on the history of British surgery and had a great passion for literature.

Jack would sit there, brow furrowed, and say, 'It's quite incredible. Who would ever think of two front-row forwards writing books?' The true front-row forward was supposed to be bone from the neck up and with his ears coming out on his shoulders. If you weren't born like that, by the time you had played rugby, that's the shape you became.

It was so good to see Pam free of pain and mobile again. She started to ride her bike, went swimming, and said tentatively, 'What about squash?'

'I should leave it just a little while,' I said. 'Certainly until the scar has healed.'

The children had all visited their mother in hospital and were at the house when she was discharged. They were standing at the door to meet her as I brought her home in the car.

There stood Trevor, Jane, Paul and Gill with a big bunch of flowers.

'We won't say "Welcome Home Mother",' said Trevor. 'We'll just say "Hip, Hip, Hooray!"'

*   *   *

We were fortunate in the spacing of our children's ages that none of them was close enough to have to compete with each other. There was three-and-a-half years between Trevor, the eldest, and Paul, and ten years between Trevor and Jane, our

41

youngest who although having two much older brothers, was neither a tomboy not spoilt. Jane developed into a good-looking, fair-haired young woman who never said a nasty word about anybody, was always a delight to have around, and was the true definition of a 'good sort'.

When I look back over my life, the best times I had were holidays with the children. The practice was good in that it allowed us to have a month in the summer so that, even when the children were quite young, we would roam all over the Continent on camping trips or get out on a boat. Even when the children had all left home, we would always try and have a few days together somewhere.

Trevor, after taking a masters' degree in law and spending a couple of years lecturing in law, went to drama school and joined the acting/writing profession which he loved. Although to date he has not become a front-line star, he has done very well and never seems to be unemployed. Part of this is because he mixes writing with acting, and mainly because he works very hard at it. If there's not much acting about, there's usually a bit of writing and vice versa. We are all of us Trevor groupies and follow him around to watch him in his various performances. To York to see him in an Alan Bleasdale play, to Southampton for a Melvyn Bragg musical. One memorable evening in London, memorable because of the heat which I thought was going to make me pass out, we sweated it out watching him play Rosencrantz and the first gravedigger in *Hamlet*, with Robert Lindsay a brilliant Hamlet.

Trevor did a bit of everything. He wrote a few episodes for *Tucker's Luck* for the BBC, as well as appearing in one. He wrote several episodes of *Albion Market* for ITV, became the Schweppes' man for the New Zealand market where he had to play a barmaid, a yokel and a butler, as well as doing commercials for Shell, some Scottish ales and various other companies.

Paul, married to the delightful Gill who painted and made jewellery, was in a job in a micro-electronics factory in Tadchester. When he had gone there initially they had given him a specifically named post and then kept on moving him sideways. He eventually finished up as a progress-chaser which is a job where everybody hates you, both the people you chase and the people who chase you.

'Never mind,' said his employers. 'If you work hard enough you will eventually become ...' and they gave the name of the job he had been originally appointed to.

Paul desperately searched round for new jobs. It would mean his leaving Tadchester, as prospects in his kind of work were limited locally. Eventually he found just the job for him in the Thames Valley. He worked for a component firm who were part of a much larger group. They really knew how to look after their employees. From the beginning Paul was encouraged: people would ring him up and say how well he was doing. He had to cover vast areas by car and spend Sundays writing reports. But most important, the firm continually encouraged and supported him, as they did all their employees. They did seem to have the art of getting the best out of people and in the nicest possible way. He enjoyed his work and was successful at it and he and Gill settled down very quickly in Berkshire.

One of the perks of the job was that Paul got a large brand-new car, a good expense account and a free telephone. It was a complete contrast to the way that he had been treated at the micro-electronics firm.

Jane was at Brighton at the polytechnic, doing a degree in the history of design. One of the criticisms of the course was that the course itself had never ever been properly designed. During the first year of her course she had only to appear two mornings a week; sometimes the lecturer didn't appear and nobody was quite sure what they were supposed to do. It would appear to an outsider that there were two careers open to you after you had completed this course. One was to write a book on how it should be done and the other was to get yourself appointed as a lecturer to tell other people what it should be about. Or shouldn't, as the case may be.

Her second year did improve. I found it all a bit confusing. Their work included photography. They went up north, visited factories, went down a coal mine and had a magnificent trip to Vienna. Jane was an industrious, interested little girl. On completing her second year it did look as if she was going to come away with a reasonable degree, whatever that was.

She loved Brighton with all its shops, the sea and the theatre. She was much more of a Trevor groupie even than we were. Trevor would always have his sister up for a few days whenever he was in a play that was running for a long time. Jane thought that when she finished her course she would like to work somewhere behind the scenes in television, theatre or radio, but that was a year or two off. First she had to get a degree.

It was a great adjustment suddenly to find it was just Pam and I in the house. We not only missed the children but we missed all the friends of the children. When Paul had been with us and his musical group was functioning, there had always been lots of young people coming and going and lots of noise and bustle. At the time it used to be a bit hard going, but how we missed it now. We felt just like Darby and Joan.

The children always came home as often as they possibly could. We always tried to make it that coming home was something they could look forward to and not an obligation. We also made trips to see Jane, to Aldermaston to call in at Paul and Gills' cottage. The only disadvantage of staying with them was that the traffic in this beautiful old Georgian village had steadily increased over the years and I could swear that from five o'clock in the morning all the heavy traffic used to come in through the bedroom window, and go out through the bathroom. I do hope that some day they will put a bypass round it. Many of the houses are three or four hundred years' old and the constant rumble of heavy goods vehicles cannot help.

General practice was time-consuming for me, and Pam, with time on her hands, now did quite a lot of work for Oxfam, had part time jobs at various times in bookshops, went to French classes and swimming with the Evergreens. I was never sure whether this was a group of people who were coloured green, some people called Evergreen, or a darling little swimming bath with a lot of foliage.

We gradually built up a life of our own together. We were fortunate that we had many good friends locally but it was difficult. There was no doubt that we'd been dependent a lot on the children. Pam felt that she was too old for camping now so our visits to the Continent would be bed-and-breakfast in inexpensive French hotels, and we found that we increasingly tried for short trips, often only two or three days and occasionally five days. We had a long weekend in Paris with our old friends Eric and his wife Zara, which included a trip on the Seine, an evening in Monmartre and inadvertently a very saucy night show which beggared description. We had river trips with Lynne and Joe Church. A trip with two new friends, Des and Joan when we took our car from Newhaven to Dieppe. A night in Beauvais with its huge cathedral and the site where the Zeppelin R101 had crashed. A wonderful day's

driving through the Compiègne forests and a night in the lovely old French family hotel in a place called Noyon which was famous in the First World War. This again had a church about as big as St Paul's Cathedral. The hotel was a lovely rambling old place; huge rooms with showers, a vast dining room with marvellous service; a meal and a bottle of wine. Our total bill each was £7 for dinner, bed and breakfast; it was unbelievable.

Then we had a trip with Primrose and Frank Squires. I had always talked about inexpensive trips to France so it was left to me to arrange a five-day trip, hopefully to explore the Loire Valley.

We spent our first night in Vitré, a town that seemed to have more churches than houses, and had a fairly indifferent meal at the hotel. The indifference of the meal was highlighted on our second night at Chinon, Rabelais' birthplace, when Pam and Frank were stricken with a tummy bug and were very ill. The only accommodation we had been able to find at Chinon was of a pretty poor standard. If you're feeling poorly and having to rush to the bathroom frequently, it's no help to your condition to see hundreds of cockroaches scuttling away every time you turn the light on. Frank was in a bad way.

'We must find a hotel with a bathroom, toilet, and telephone,' he said. 'I don't think I'm going to survive this trip.'

We went on to Tours and after a lot of wandering round, found a magnificent hotel. It was not too expensive, and had beautiful marble staircases, plush rooms with every facility under the sun. It was a lovely summer's day and the streets were filled with market stalls, including many outside cafes. We ventured out in the evening — those that were eating, that is — to one of these kerbside cafes for kebabs.

This trip was some sort of record in that during the five days that we were away there was no single meal that all of us were fit enough to eat together. On the first night it had been Primrose with a migraine. On the second night George and Pam. Then intermittently until we got home, there was always one at each meal who dined solely on Perrier water. From

Tours we moved on to St Malo where Frank recovered but Pam still seemed a bit shaky. It was Primrose's birthday on our second night there and Frank had found a magnificent restaurant where, apart from Pam, we all did justice to our meal.

I always go armed with a pharmacopoeia of medicines when we go abroad. I don't know how people manage without them. Certainly this trip would have been a disaster if I hadn't been able to supply the appropriate drugs. In the end we all put it down as a great experience. We put the hotel in Virtré into the Bad Food Guide that we were compiling and arrived home safely, all of us a bit thinner but none of us too much the worse for wear.

*   *   *

Pam half promised that when I retired, which wasn't in the too far distant future, she and I might do a bit of camping again together. When we had camped with the children, often with our friends Margaret and Sally as well, the car was usually so jam-packed with things that we could hardly move. Now we felt that with just the two of us, a tent and a few cooking things and sleeping bags thrown in, would be enough.

Neither of us were big eaters. Lunches in France were always a set routine. First a village where we could buy pâté, a bottle of wine, some cheese; next a river bank in the sunshine, preferably with a nice shady tree nearby. There are very few pleasures better than being stretched out on the river bank in the sunshine after your bread, pâté, sausage and cheese, washed down with half a bottle of wine and a cup of coffee boiled on the little gas stove. An extra treat was a French cigar called a Voltagar which although about ten times the size, was the same price as a cigarette. There was a picture of a camel on the front of the packet: Eric said it was unique in being the only packet which carried a picture of the animal that produced the material for the tobacco.

Yes, we loved France. Not that in any way we didn't love England, but France had one particular more or less guaranteed ingredient that if you went far enough south you could always find what we lacked. Sunshine.

* * *

Pam and I decided to spoil ourselves with an expensive holiday. We chose Madeira, which I had visited once before and had always hoped to take Pam to, and which many of our friends talked of as some sort of paradise.

We flew out on a cold February morning and landed at this delightful island noted for its short runway which limited the size of planes that could land there. Traditionally, all the passengers cheered as the pilot landed the plane safely.

We were driven to the best hotel I have stayed at in my life. The towels in the room were changed twice a day. This worried me so much that I used to go and dampen unused towels just to show the room attendant how clean I was. There was a large swimming pool, surrounded by lawn, with special couches to lounge on. And a man assigned to carry your mattress and towel and make you comfortable on your couch. I would hate to be called a sybarite, but this was heaven.

It was a pleasant walk down to Funchal, which had not been spoilt by tourists. The indigenous population had held its own. There was a marvellous fish market, an abundance of flowers, some lovely old buildings and pleasant places to sit out in the sun having coffee and just watching people go by.

The hotel had been designed by the same architect who designed Brasilia and he had designed it on the same scale. You entered the restaurant, with room for a thousand diners, down a huge sweeping ramp to a vast room surrounded by windows about forty feet high.

There's an old cliché about its being a small world. There's a more recent one about not being able to take your mistress anywhere these days. Wherever you go, however far from home, you're bound to bump into somebody you know.

As Pam and I sat down to our first meal, a lady from the next table got up and said, 'Isn't it Dr Clifford?'

It was Jean Davis who used to be the health visitor in

Tadchester, staying there with another health visitor friend. On the plane coming over we met the local baronet from Tadchester, who came over every winter and spent a month at Reid's Hotel, in the same room. He said he had come specifically this year to practise tying his flies. Being a bit slow on the uptake, and especially as I knew he hadn't been well, I thought for heaven's sake, why doesn't he buy himself a zip? But of course he meant tying his flies for his fly fishing. It just shows the mess you can get into when you are not properly brought up.

There were a number of trips around the island. We went up to see the extinct volcanic crater, which was superb. We did a toboggan ride down the streets with men in immaculate white flannels, jumping on either side of the sledge to stop us bumping into the walls. We saw the woods, and on the far side the massive waterfalls which provided Madeira with its hydro-electricity.

There were little sheds that held cows, not for milk, but purely as producers of manure: all dairy products were imported. The cows were fed on any old rubbish and usually spent a lifetime in the shed, becoming blind. There was just not sufficient land for grazing, and I did feel rather sorry for the poor old cows.

On one of our trips round the island the guide told us the various theories of how Madeira had originated. One theory was that it was part of the lost island of Atlantis that was still sticking above the water. Another was that it was part of a volcanic eruption and one of a series of islands including the Canaries. The third theory was that when God made the world, he was so pleased with what he had done that he bent down and kissed the sea. Where he kissed the sea Madeira was formed. I must say I went along with that.

Most of the hotels had nightclubs, not sophisticated hot-spots, but pleasant genteel places where middle-aged couples, like ourselves, could waltz to *Who's Taking You Home Tonight?* and other tunes of our vintage.

One of the main problems was that every time we went out to a nightclub it seemed to coincide with the night starring the

Portuguese dancers, who pulled out members of the audience to join in their very vigorous dancing. I almost carried a notice saying, 'Beware Portuguese dancers'.

By sheer chance, we had chosen carnival week in Madeira, the island's most important week of the year.

We were treated to the spectacle of mile after mile of beautifully clad young men and women dancing to bands that bobbed up about every fifth or sixth group. They wore the most exotic and bizarre costumes: giraffes, swans, toadstools, bananas and apples. Our own hotel's group, dressed as shell-fish — lobsters, prawns and crabs — won first prize. It was a magic night with bonfires lighting up this procession of happy, beautifully-dressed young people and cheering crowds.

The carnival lasted all week and the main hotels were visited each evening by the carnival dancers. The judging of costumes took place in our hotel in the massive dining room which was cleared of all the tables. There was dancing all night, or at least there was moving about to music on the packed floor.

The hotel doors were flung wide open, at least five thousand strangers poured into the hotel, and although quite a number of people had had a few drinks, I didn't see a single drunk.

Nothing was stolen from the hotel, nothing was damaged. Even stranger still, there wasn't a single policeman in sight. It was a tremendous tribute to how things can be, and I hope it never changes. It was a place where ladies could safely go on holiday on their own, could walk the streets safely at night. Madeira is a small island, admittedly, and there is nowhere for a robber to run to, but it was very refreshing to spend just a short time in this unsophisticated atmosphere.

There was just one incident that cast a gloom on the holiday. The lady sitting next to me on the plane coming over was confused about her papers. She was a lady in her late seventies. I asked if I could help, and it came out that I was a doctor.

'I'm so pleased to know that there's a doctor,' she said, and she was even more pleased to know that I was going to her hotel.

I asked how much she had travelled in the past.

'I've never travelled alone on my own before. This is my first flight and my first trip abroad.'

She then gave me an account of the medication she was on. She suffered from severe heart disease and was diabetic. My heart sank. It looked as if I was going to have a patient for the whole week, but she was such a nice person and it had been her life's ambition to come to Madeira to see the orchids.

She was part of a singles group and we were pleased to see, on the first evening at dinner, that she was at a table with about thirty other people, all chatting. We didn't see her at all the next day but on the following day Pam and I found her sitting looking rather exhausted in the hall. We chatted to her briefly. She had seen her orchids and was rather tired, just taking a rest before going up to her room.

At dinner, she came in halfway through the meal and sat down alone. We determined to take her under our wing, so Jean Davis, her friend Marjorie, Pam and I went over and asked her to join us for coffee. We had a lovely evening with her, and she told us all about her family: how her daughter hadn't wanted her to go on her own, and how they were all worried about her.

In spite of us seeing her with about thirty people on the first night, she had been having a pretty lonely time. She had walked up the hill by herself from Funchal, and that had nearly killed her, but she had seen her Madeira orchids and fulfilled her lifelong ambition.

She was good company. What she hadn't seen was the hotel, so Jean Davis, who was the best of good souls, said she would pick her up from her room in the morning to show her around, and she would travel with us in future.

Next morning Jean came to me by the pool and said, 'It's very strange, there's a notice saying "Do Not Disturb" outside the old lady's room and they won't let me in. It's all very mysterious.'

I went down to the manager and told him that we were looking for our friend and couldn't understand why there was no reply. He looked at me and asked me into his office.

'Excuse me, sir, but did you know the lady in No 10?'

'Yes,' I said. 'Quite well. We spent yesterday evening with her.'

'I'm afraid I have some very bad news for you,' he said. 'She died in her sleep last night.'

This was absolutely staggering. We had had such a happy time the previous evening. She had told us about seeing the marvellous orchids which had fulfilled a life's ambition. I was able to ring her daughter who was absolutely distraught. She had obviously been a mum who was adored by her family. They were worried to death about her going in the physical state she was in but, she had insisted that before she died she would see her Madeira orchids.

Her condition was such that she could have gone at any time. Similarly she could have staggered on for a few years, but there must have been some instinct which told her that her time was short and unless she did the thing she had always wanted to do, she might never do it. In spite of her poor health, and in spite of never travelling by air before, she had the courage to get up and go. Suddenly I wasn't sad any more, just proud to have known this most courageous little lady who had achieved her lifetime's ambition.

CHAPTER 6

Clanger Bartlett

Clanger Bartlett arrived suddenly out of the blue. We had a phone call to say that he was in Plymouth. Could he come and see us?

I hadn't seen Clanger since my student days when he had been one of my closest friends, completing a trio with Taffy Williams, now a very distinguished physician in Scotland. Somehow, although we were very different characters, we stuck together all through our student years.

Taffy was brilliant: as well as qualifying in medicine he took an Honours Physiology Degree, topping the pass list at London University. Clanger was a mature student and had been doing some laboratory work before taking up medicine, and was more sophisticated and worldly-wise than Taffy or myself. He had easily assumed the name 'Clanger' because he could put his foot in it more times than any other six people put together. He was accident-prone but a good and loyal friend.

Without Taffy and Clanger I would have never survived or even qualified in medicine. Clanger and I both failed our second MB . . . mine through spending too much time at rugby and not being very bright, and Clanger through his variety of interests. He always had several different hobbies on the go and now, true to form, he flew his own plane and collected vintage Rolls-Royces.

He and I, after failing our second MB together, sweated through the whole of one summer in my mother's flat in Chelsea, being coached by Taffy. Taffy, as London's star physiology student, somehow managed to help his two mates scramble through at their second attempt.

We both qualified eventually, Clanger staying on at our teaching hospital to work in the pathology laboratories, then spending some years in Canada before returning to work in the midlands, and more recently doing some work with the Armed Forces.

The memory of two occasions with Clanger still brings me out in a cold sweat. One weekend the three of us took my mother's boat out on the Thames. The boat was called *Avise* and it had the special characteristic of having two lots of controls, that is to say two throttles. One was near the steering wheel and the other, which controlled the reversing mechanism only, at the back.

With Clanger steering, we were coming up to a lock somewhere near Hampton Court. A whole row of boats was queuing to go in, but Clanger thought he saw an empty space at the head of the queue. He throttled forward and the boat shot past the waiting line. Seeing the danger from my post at the back, I put the boat full astern. Astern won; we crashed into the lock approach wall and smashed our rudder in half, to the delight of the several hundred spectators who were coming out of Sandown Park races.

Somehow we managed to patch the boat up and limp back to its moorings. Taffy, who had nothing at all to do with the disaster, followed it by a week in bed with severe sunstroke. 'There just isn't any justice,' he groaned.

The *Avise* had a very strange history. It was reported to have crossed the Channel, which I can't believe. My mother had bought it ostensibly to hire it out but it was a pretty scruffy old boat. She did have one reply to her advertisement. A young, very unmarried-looking, couple wanted to hire the boat for a week. My mother was explaining how they should approach locks, what they did in locks, and what they did after locks, but they didn't seem to take much notice. She repeated her instructions and then said, 'You do understand about locks?'

'Don't worry,' they said confidently. 'We're not going to bother with locks – we're going to go round them.'

There was a panic call from them after they had been out for three days to say that they had broken down in front of an oncoming steamer and had abandoned the boat way up river. My mother and I had to go up and fetch it back.

Another fine mess Clanger got me into, or one I got him into, was a boxing match against Cambridge University. By failing to attend a meeting I came down one day to find I was the secretary of the boxing club and responsible for organising boxing fixtures. Failing to attend another meeting of boxing secretaries, I found I had been appointed vice-captain of the United Hospital Boxing Club, and my first job was to organise a match.

I was quite inexperienced with these things and had difficulty in finding a hall, particularly one with seats in. I eventually found one at the Elephant and Castle that had no seats. Full of resource, I borrowed some folding chairs from a nearby church hall, but had to erect them all as well as pick up and return them.

We had been sent the team list of the Cambridge boxers. I was selected to fight the Cambridge secretary and to my horror I found I was two pounds above the lightweight limit. (It is a very sobering thought to think that nowadays I would be fighting as a heavyweight.) In spite of all the rushing about and preparations for the match, I still had to spend the afternoon in a Turkish bath to lose the two surplus pounds.

I got to the hall to find that my opponent had been unable to come. We were very short of bouts, so to make up numbers I agreed reluctantly to fight their middleweight boxing blue. It was not an over-long bout. He knocked me out in the first round as well as knocking a piece off one of my teeth. My bank

manager, who was an old family friend, had come out to the Elephant and Castle to watch all this. He was very impressed. As he told my mother: 'Bob was fighting very well until he got knocked out.'

We just managed to scramble enough bouts together to provide the local, very roughnecked, crowd with an evening's entertainment. I showered after my knockout, dressed and came into the hall to find a man in a dark suit waiting for me. He was from the Customs and Excise, for which I should apparently have made some provision, and he assured me they would summons me after the match was over.

We had to wait until everybody had gone to clear the hall and take the chairs in Clanger's mother's brand-new car back to the church hall. At last we set off home. Clanger was a man of sudden impulses. We were driving back though London at the head of a queue of traffic when, within about two feet of a pedestrian crossing, Clanger decided to stop to let an old lady cross. Without any warning he jammed on his brakes. A lorry ran into the back of him and a car ran into the back of the lorry. It was the end of a perfect day.

I went with Clanger to explain to his mother the crumpled appearance of the back of her brand-new car. She was very good about it. This was at the time when getting any sort of car was a premium and a new one was like gold dust.

Before Clanger's visit to us at Tadchester, he had been involved in the setting up of a specialised blood unit, of which there was only one in England and one in America. He had travelled down to London for a course of instruction due to start on a Friday, only to find that the specialist had gone to America for the weekend, and that the lecture would not be until Monday. The lecturer appeared on Monday dishevelled, exhausted and unshaven, but somehow got through the lecture. Clanger tackled him on his absence the previous Friday and was given the following explanation:

A Saudi Arabian businessman, said the lecturer, had come to him with a blood disorder. He examined the businessman's blood and said he would need some special type of blood replacement which was only done at one place in England.

'Good,' said the Saudi. 'Ring them and fix it up.'

The specialist rang to find that the only six private beds in this hospital were full. The only way the Saudi could go in was as a National Health patient. The hospital, like many old English hospitals was archaic, just about falling down and desperately in need of funds.

'Right,' said the Saudi. 'Ring them back and say that I will donate a million dollars to the hospital if a private bed can be found for me.'

The consultant rang back. Whoever was in charge of beds there said the money would not make the slightest difference. The Saudi Arabian could come in as a National Health patient or not at all. He was quite happy to let a million dollars slip through the hospital's fingers.

'Where else could I get this done?' asked the Saudi.

'There's only one other place, and that's in North America,' said our consultant.

'Right,' said the Saudi. 'Fix it up there.'

This was done in a few minutes with a transatlantic phone call.

'There's only one condition that I insist on before agreeing to go there,' said the Saudi. 'And that is that you accompany me. I am of course prepared to donate a large sum to your research unit here for this service.'

So the bedraggled physician had to commute to North America once a week to attend his wealthy patient, who happily made a good recovery.

I told this story to a prominent London businessman who was holidaying in Tadchester. He had come across the same kind of situation. A multi-million pound deal had been arranged at government level with some Middle Eastern potentate. Almost as they sat down to sign the agreement, as an afterthought the Middle Eastern gentleman said, 'By the way, I would like my son to be found a place,' naming a well known British university. The university was consulted but were unable to offer a place other than through the usual academic channels. However, Harvard University in the States, acted quite differently when approached. They were only too delighted to give a place to the son, and both the boy and the multi-million dollar contract went to America.

There are two morals to be drawn from these stories. I have never ever been able to work out which is the right one.

CHAPTER 7

Dimming Lights

I am always saddened to note the onset of senility in my older patients. Usually the process is a gradual one, but sometimes it can strike with startling rapidity and within a few months turn an intelligent, lucid and responsible person into a shambling, incoherent baby.

Geordie Napier was one who changed quickly. He was a retired miner, whippety but strong as an ox, whose great delight was to tell of the famous fight he had underground long ago with four other miners.

'Whipped the lot of 'em,' he'd boast, crouching into a boxer's stance and jabbing at the air with his fists. 'One after the other.'

When senility set in, the story became confused and rambling, and the number of his opponents expanded into dozens. Sometimes he would revert right back to childhood and sing nursery songs, or tell schoolkid jokes and snigger at the more risqué ones.

Geordie's wife, Rose, had the patience of a saint. She washed him, dressed him, fed him and tolerated calmly all his silly ways. 'He's been a good husband to me,' she'd say. 'Never drank. Always brought his pay packet home unopened. The least I can do is look after him now.'

But the strain on Rose began to tell. Geordie didn't sleep a lot, so the poor woman was on the go practically twenty hours a day. To give her a break, I pulled strings to get Geordie into the old people's home for a fortnight.

It was a great weight off Rose's mind for a couple of weeks, but a great trial for the staff at the old folks' home. Every day, Geordie caused ructions, usually finishing by putting up his fists and challenging all comers to a re-enactment of his famous victory down the pit.

One day there was a special treat for the old people — a mystery tour by coach, with a pub lunch at the destination, a market town about forty miles from Tadchester. Geordie was included on the trip; not the wisest decision the home's administrators ever made.

He behaved himself on the trip out, and through the pub lunch. Then he had a half pint of beer ... the first alcoholic drink of his life at nearly eighty. He found it very much to his liking, so much so that he sidled off into another bar and bought himself a whole pint from the spending money the home had provided.

When the time came to leave, Geordie was nowhere to be found. Panic set in among the organisers of the trip, and they went in search of him. They didn't have far to look.

Under a bridge over the river in the centre of the town, a bunch of down-and-outs spent their days drinking cider mixed with meths. They generally followed their pursuit quietly, and the police let them get on with it. But when the searchers arrived there was a huge commotion going on, with a policeman trying to restore order among the brawling drunks.

In the centre of the melée was Geordie, prancing about on his toes and squaring up to the enormous bobby.

'He's harmless!' shouted one of the search party. 'We'll take him home!'

'Harmless?' said the copper. 'Look what he's done to *them*!'

There, on the ground, lay two of the drunks — out to the wide, laid low in Geordie's Last Stand.

It turned out that Geordie had left the pub, roaring drunk

on the small amount of beer, and entertained the methies with a couple of songs and some jokes. They had rewarded him with swigs from their cider bottles, which led to a garbled account — with actions — of the fight underground. A couple of drunks had misunderstood and had gone for Geordie. That was a mistake, as the prostrate forms on the ground testified. The other drunks had taken sides, and within seconds a general free-for-all had broken out, alarming enough for the police to be called.

'OK then,' said the policeman, grabbing Geordie by the shoulders and lifting him clear off the ground, 'Take him away – but for God's sake, never bring him back ...'

*   *   *

Tommy Butcher was a self-educated former trade union leader, a highly intelligent man, and in his day a tough and shrewd negotiator, feared by management. His senility was strangely intermittent: he'd be speaking quite lucidly and logically one minute, then suddenly lapse into gibberish. He'd return to normality and realise that his mind had been wandering. This happened during one of my visits: after three or four minutes of talking pure nonsense, Tommy snapped back into his normal state of mind and suddenly burst into tears.

'Excuse that, Doctor,' he said, blowing into his handkerchief. 'It's not often I've cried in my life. But it's one thing to be going barmy, and quite another to know it. I just wish now I could stay potty all the time ... '

*　　*　　*

The most startling change was in old Winnie Parsons. She'd had a hard life bringing up five children on her fisherman husband's small income. She'd always kept them, her house, and herself spotless. She was a neat, tidy woman, very reserved, highly respectable and a keen churchgoer.

In her late seventies, and within the space of a few months, she changed completely. She became slovenly and foul-mouthed, even to the extent of bawling obscenities in church. She was suspicious of everyone around her, including her devoted husband, whom she accused of all kinds of infidelities and foul practices. She failed to recognise her grandchildren, and finally failed to recognise her husband.

'Who *is* this man?' she'd yell when he came into the room. 'Take him away! Dirty bastard! Don't let him touch me!'

Within nine months from the onset, Winnie was dead.

I hate losing a patient, and take the deaths of even the old ones to heart, but in Winnie's case I made an exception. Without putting any finer point on it she was, poor old thing, better off dead.

*　　*　　*

And yet other patients moved into old age with dignity, even with zest. Nellie Walters was one. After the death of her husband, Nellie emigrated to Australia to join her daughter and son-in-law. Lots of people emigrate to Australia, but few at the age of eighty-two.

Within two years, Winnie was back.

'What was the matter?' I asked, when she called at the surgery. 'Didn't things work out?'

'Oh, I got on well enough with my daughter and her family,' said Winnie. 'Always did. They made me very welcome, and bought a mobile home for me with all mod cons and set it up in their garden so that I could have my own place.

'But Australia takes some getting used to. Their garden for a start – huge, it was. Seemed like acres and acres. But it had acres and acres of *dust*. For nine months of the year there wasn't a blade of grass in sight.

'And creepy-crawlies! Spiders, centipedes, horrible big beetles – they had the lot. Never could stand creepy-crawlies of any kind, let alone giant ones.

'The heat, too. Most of the time I was either in the shower or lying on my bed with the electric fan full on, trying to keep cool. Too much at my time of life.'

'I can see why you came back, Nellie,' I said. 'Don't think I'd fancy that very much!'

'No, I don't think you would. Take my word for it. But what finally did it was Danish bacon!'

'Danish bacon? Didn't you like it?'

'Love it. But that was the trouble – in Australia you couldn't get it, and Australian bacon isn't a patch on it. I was like that old man in *Treasure Island* – or was it *Robinson Crusoe*? – the one who dreamt of cheese all the time. I'd lie awake at nights thinking of Danish bacon, sizzling away in the pan. In the end, I'd had enough and got the boat back home. And the first thing I had when I got off at Southampton was a huge plate of Danish bacon.'

'Great, Nellie,' I said. 'And now what can I do for you?'

'Indigestion mixture, Doctor,' she said. 'The kind you used to give me. Since I've been back I've been over-eating. And do you remember that anything fatty used to bring on my acid?'

'Ah yes,' I said. 'Anything fatty used to do that. Such as – '

'You don't need to tell me,' said Nellie. 'Such as Danish
bacon . . .'

*   *   *

I worried about the health of Ida Allsopp, though she brought
many of her ailments upon herself. She lived in a small cottage
near the river and refused to leave it. She and her husband
had spent long and happy years there and after his death she
felt it would be a disloyalty to give up their old home.

But the place had stone-flagged floors, no proper damp
course, and was consequently cold and wet. It was draughty
too, as Ida's old landlord didn't have the funds to keep the
place in good order.

Ida was bronchitic, and there was no hope of her ever
getting better so long as she lived in that cottage. But all my

pleas for her to move, all my offers to help get her an old people's flat, had no effect whatsoever.

Then the council bought the cottage for modernisation. The renovation was to be so extensive that there was no way Ida could stay while work was in progress. She was moved out, protesting loudly, to a purpose-built block of old people's council flats near the parish church. 'Just for a few weeks, love,' the social worker explained. 'And when your cottage is done up, you can move back in.'

'Oh, all right,' said Ida, grumpily. 'But I'm not staying in that new place a day longer than I have to.'

The flats were marvellous. Centrally heated, lifts to every floor, ultra-modern kitchens and, best of all, a series of alarm bells on the walls at different heights, so that any old person in trouble could ring for the warden who looked after the flats.

After a few days grumbling, Ida got accustomed to her new surroundings and began to take an interest in them. One window overlooked the grounds of the parish church, a blaze of colour in summer with the well-tended rose beds. Another overlooked a shopping precinct and several pubs, so that there was always human activity for Ida to look out at. The precinct meant, too, that many of Ida's old friends would call on her when they'd done their day's shopping, so she was never short of company.

One day Ida collapsed with a heart attack. As she lay on the floor she had the presence of mind to press the alarm button in the skirting board. In less than a minute the warden was up in the lift and opening the flat door with his pass-key. A quick 999 call, and the ambulance was round.

Ida recovered, and eventually the time came for her to move back into her old cottage.

'If it's all the same to you,' she told the social worker, 'I'd rather stay here.'

'That's all right, love,' said the social worker. 'No problem. But you do surprise me, especially now that the old place is snug and warm.'

'Right,' said Ida. 'But I used to sit there for weeks and never see a soul. Here I see people every day – with a free show every night, too, when the pubs turn out.

'And I'm not daft enough to think I may never have another heart attack. Just think – if I was still living in that cottage I'd be dead.'

'Half a minute,' said the social worker, dazed by Ida's logic. 'I'll need time to work that one out . . .'

CHAPTER 8

Fishing Lessons

I don't number fishing among my more highly developed skills, but I do enjoy it, especially when I can get out with John Denton for a day and learn a bit more about it.

Enjoyment is a big part of John's philosophy.

'We're only here once, lad,' he'd say. 'Se we'd best make the most of it. That cemetery over there is full of miserable buggers wishing they'd laughed a bit more when they had the chance.'

Which was one reason John didn't have much time for the matchmen who crowded the banks of the Tad during the coarse fishing season, at least not for the obsessive ace matchmen whose only aim was to win at all costs.

'The lads themselves are all right,' he said. 'They don't take it too seriously, have a few laughs, and look forward to wetting their whistles and telling lies in the pub afterwards. There's more to fishing than catching fish. But some of the top rankers in the Tadchester A Team make your hair stand on end.

'Winning is all they're bothered about. They've got tackle that cost a king's ransom. Secret baits that twenty-four hours on the rack wouldn't get out of them. They're snooping round the club, earwigging in the pubs, in the hope of picking up any scraps of information about the water that would help them win a prize. They play merry hell about the peg draw if they've been given a bad swim to fish. And if they don't come first at the weigh-in they're jumping up and down and demanding a re-weigh.

'They're skilled all right: you've got to give them that. Snatching tiddlers at a rate you wouldn't believe. But they don't need *fish* – they'd be just as happy being let loose with a swatter in a room full of flies and seeing who could swat the most. Aye, it might be clever, but I'm buggered if it's fishing.'

Certainly the matchmen weren't happy during August. The weather had been hot and dry for several weeks, the river was low and de-oxygenated, and the fish were refusing to co-operate.

'Not much chance for me, then, John,' I said.

'I don't know, lad. If you fancy it, we can try tomorrow away from the match stretches. Apart from anything else, those match lengths are so soured by untouched groundbait that they'll be fit for nothing until the water starts moving again. We'll have a go for gudgeon.'

'Gudgeon, John? But that's tiddler-snatching, surely?'

'Don't you believe it. Get a gudgeon on light tackle and you'll feel him all right. No Moby Dick, I grant you, but for his size he's the best scrapper in the river. There's a bloke in Ireland, runs fishing holidays on the River Blackwater, who actually advertises gudgeon among the attractions – and that's in Ireland, where fishing really *is* fishing.'

The gudgeon is a small fish – though it has been known to grow to half a pound, the British rod-caught record is only 4 oz 4 drams – and it's not very pretty. It's a speckled grey or greeny-brown, and grubs around the bottom feeling for food with two little barbels that hang down from either side of its mouth like a droopy moustache. I'd heard no end of jokes about it among anglers in the Tadchester Arms, ribbing each other about gudgeon which fought like tigers.

'Aye, they're a joke when there are bigger fish stirring,' said John. 'But in weather like this, when other fish are off their grub, the gudgeon will go on feeding. And not only will they give you a run for your money on light tackle: if you hit a decent-sized shoal you could pull in fifty-odd fish in a morning. It's all right those blokes pretending to look down on the gudgeon, but they're bloody glad of them when there's nowt else about.'

Next morning we got down to the river just as the sun was lifting the mist from the water. John led the way to a long, gentle bay which cut into clear bank between two stretches of trees.

He pegged out two keepnets in the shallow water, supporting the end of each with a couple of old rod rests to make sure the mesh would not fold back to trap the fish, should we be lucky enough to catch any. Then he walked to the nearest clump of trees and returned with an armful of leafy twigs.

'What are those for, John? Camouflage?'

'Nay, lad. Shade,' he said, poking the ends of the twigs under the wire frames of the keepnets. 'They'll keep the sun off the nets. Strong sunshine in shallow water doesn't do the fish a lot of good. And once they're in the net, there's nowhere they can go to find shade.'

We then set our landing nets.

'A bit ambitious, aren't we, John?'

'Not really. We could just swing the fish in without a net, but it doesn't do them a lot of good. May as well do the job properly from the start, even if it does look a bit daft.'

We each tackled up with a fragile-looking nine-foot rod, a reel holding almost invisible nylon line with a breaking strain of only one pound, a No 14 hook and a float of the tiniest quill.

From his rod holdall, John produced a garden rake.

'I didn't like to ask before,' I said. 'But what the hell's that for? You're not doing a bit of gardening on the side?'

'You'll see,' said John. 'Tried and trusted is this.'

He waded out slowly into the shallow, slow-running water, taking care not to splash, and raked the bottom in two patches, about twenty feet apart, back towards the bank. Mud and bits of debris swirled to the surface and turned the water into the colour and consistency of thick cocoa.

'That'll attract 'em' he said. 'Nothing they like better than a pea-souper, full of creepy-crawlies from out of the mud.'

We each baited up with a tiny red worm, of which John had brought along a tinful, harvested from his compost heap, cast out and waited for the first twitch on the floats. We made our usual bets: 5p on the first fish, 5p on the biggest and 5p on the most. Beauregard Denton and Ace-High Clifford, last of the Mississippi gamblers.

We sat there for fifteen minutes or so without a tremble on the quills. John walked over to throw some chopped meat and bits of worm around my float.

'What's up, John? Reckon even the gudgeon are giving it a miss today?'

'No. They'll be around all right. Almost certainly rooting around there now. A bit of extra grub will encourage them to – Hey up!'

He strode swiftly back to his own rod and struck with a quick turn of the wrist. The top of the light rod jagged wildly as the fish plunged this way and that. Within a few seconds he had drawn the fish over the top of his landing net and was lifting it clear of the water.

He unhooked it, first wetting his hand so as not to strip it of its slime, and brought it over to show me: a muddy-looking, unprepossessing little thing, but a fish, nevertheless. He put it into the keepnet with as much care as if it were a prizewinning Japanese ornamental carp.

'You're a witness, Bob,' he said. 'Fought like a tiger. That's 5p to me then. *We're in the money ...* '

As I was laughing at John, my own float trembled violently and shot under the surface. I struck, a little late but still in time, and was rewarded by a fierce thrumming on the rod. I was sure I'd hooked the world's record, and was disappointed at the size of the tiny fish which had caused all the excitement.

'Told you, didn't I?' said John. 'If these grew bigger, nobody would fish for anything else.'

The morning progressed very pleasantly in a drowsy hum of insects. It was reasonably cool on the bank, although the sun beat down relentlessly from a cloudless sky. Every five minutes or so, one or both of us would have a bite. Each time there was that amazingly fierce throbbing on the light rod; each time the appearance of a fish four or five inches long that looked as if it shouldn't have been parted from its mother.

When things got slack, John would wade gently out, give the bottom another rake, and throw in more chopped meat and bits of worm around the floats. Before long, back came the fish; usually when I wasn't ready for them.

They had an uncanny knack of taking my float under just as I was in the middle of taking the top off the thermos flask or opening a packet of sandwiches. This resulted in a few missed strikes and some muttered curses. (Non-gambler though I am, 5p is 5p.) One sure way of getting a bite was to leave the rod to answer a call of nature. When I got back, there was the float diving underwater and surfacing again as the fish dropped the bait.

71

Eventually, along came twelve noon.

'Right, lad. That's it,' said John. 'They've stopped biting now.'

'Never on your life. Hang on. I had a twitch then.'

'You know the rules, Bob,' said John. 'At twelve noon they stop biting. Go dead off their feed. Any twitches on the float are purely an optical illusion.'

I knew the rules. At twelve noon John packed up, giving himself plenty of time to get over to the Tadchester Arms for his one o'clock pint. A creature of habit, our John.

We lifted out the keepnets and counted the fish. I'd done well with forty-four; John had done better with sixty-three.

'Another 5p to me,' said John. 'But I've got to give you best for the biggest fish. Look at that little beauty of yours.'

The little beauty was three ounces if it were a dram; a giant among gudgeon. So even though my feckless gambling had left me 5p down, I could still boast of having caught the biggest fish of the day – and that fishing against the bailiff himself.

'Make a nice fry-up' said John, as he carefully slid the fish back into the water.

'I wouldn't fancy them,' I said, looking at the mud-coloured backs wriggling swiftly beneath the surface.

'You would,' said John. 'Great Victorian delicacy, these. They used to have punt parties, with everybody – women and all – fishing for gudgeon. And then they'd have big fry–ups on the bank. Butter, flour, few herbs, salt and pepper, squeeze of lemon: delicious. Only trouble is you need a lot of them for a plateful. Poor little buggers.'

In the Tadchester Arms we met another angler, hunched gloomily over the bar.

'Any luck?' asked John.

'Not a sausage. Not a nibble. You two?'

'Sixty-three for me,' said John. 'And forty-four for Bob here.'

'Give over. Sixty-three what?'

'Gudgeon.'

'Gudgeon? *Gudgeon*? Who wants bloody gudgeon?'

'Better than nowt,' said John, slurping gratefully into his pint. 'At least we've not come back looking as if we've been to a bloody funeral.'

'There's more to fishing than catching fish,' said the angler.

'You never said a truer word,' said John. 'Cheers.'

*   *   *

'Remember the gudgeon?' asked John, one October evening.

'I ought to,' I said. 'Who was it won 5p on the biggest fish?'

'Aye, well, there's another fish that's despised by some. The grayling, one of the most beautiful fish that swims. We'll try for some tomorrow, if you like.'

'You're on. But how come it's despised if it's so beautiful?'

'Strictly speaking it's a game fish, a member of the salmon family just like the salmon and trout. But a lot of upmarket game fishermen look down on it because it spawns at the same time as the coarse fish. Bit *infra dig*, dontcha know. To protect it, it's covered by the coarse close season rather than the game close season. And that puts it right outside the pale for the old pukka sahibs.

'Anyway, we'll try for some tomorrow. Bring some float trotting gear and a fly rod as well.'

The next morning was a glorious start to the day, with the leaves taking on their first flush of autumnal red and gold.

'Best time of the year for me, is autumn,' said John. 'And it's the best time for coarse fish – begging the grayling's pardon. They're well over spawning, they've muscled up and they're in good fighting trim.'

John stopped on the river at a smooth, fast run, and cast an eye over the water.

'Now then, we could trot down with worm. We'll have to do that to find the fish if they're feeding below the surface. But – Aye, there we go –' John broke off at a splash and a swirl downstream – 'they're taking at the surface, so we'll try dry fly. Do you no harm, anyway: you've not done much fly work this year.'

We both assembled our nine-foot trout rods and put a flashy dry fly on the point of the line.

'The trick is,' said John, 'to cast downstream and across. With a dry fly you'd normally cast upstream, but the grayling has very keen eyesight, so we want the fly to reach it before it spots the line. Make sure you give line once you've cast; you don't want the fly to be affected by the drag. Go on – after you.'

I cast to land just upstream of where the splash had been. The fly floated down and then – whoosh! – another splash, and a swirl. But the fly went drifting on, untouched.

'Reel in and cast again at the same spot,' said John. 'Grayling are messy risers, another reason the game wallahs aren't always keen on them. They sometimes shoot straight from the bottom and miss the fly altogether.'

I cast out again. Another swirl and – Strike!

'Missed!' I howled as the fly was flicked clear of the water.

'No panic,' said John. 'The grayling is accused of having a soft mouth which allows the hook to come out easily. But it hasn't: it's got a small mouth and it nips rather than swallows. This time let it take the fly and turn under, then strike with just a turn of the wrist.'

I followed John's instructions and – Gottim!

'By heck, John, this is a scrapper,' I stuttered as my rod bucked and curved.

'Aye, well, you're taking her back against the current and she's got a dorsal fin like a sail to take full advantage of it. You'll see when you get her out.'

I played the fish upstream back almost to the bank. John slid the landing net into the water.

'Gently does it now, Bob,' he whispered. 'These things have a habit of kicking as they come to the net. Shame to lose her after all this.'

I lifted the rod tip so that the fish's head just cleared the surface, and slid it sideways over the net.

'Hup!' grunted John. And there was my first grayling.

What a fish! What a beauty!

The silver of its flanks was shot through with iridescent tones of purple, indigo, green and yellow, making it shimmer like watered silk. Its fins were tinged with purple. And most magnificent of all was its stately dorsal fin, shaped like an artist's palette, an impression which was heightened by its shimmering purple tones and the dark horizontal bands which ran across it.

I looked at the fish in the net for a full minute before starting to take the hook out.

'I don't think I've seen anything quite so beautiful,' I said.

'No, you'd go a long way to beat that,' said John.

'But if you don't take that hook out soon, you'll have nowt to look at. Those colours fade once the fish dies. Straight back in the water, lad: we don't want to risk that fin a keepnet. We could eat her, of course, but if you saw those colours fade it'd put you right off your grub.'

I wetted my hands, took the hook out, and turned to the water.

'One second, Bob,' said John. 'Smell her.'

'What for?'

'Just smell her.'

I sniffed.

What does she smell like?'

'Fish.'

'Good. She's supposed to smell of thyme. In fact her Latin name is *Thymallus thymallus*. But to me she's always smelled like fish. For years I thought I was missing something.'

'There she goes,' I said as I slid the fish back into the water. 'Little beauty, wasn't she? You've got me at it now, John, calling the thing "she".'

'Only seems right with a thing as beautiful as that,' said John. 'You couldn't imagine her being called Fred or Sid, could you? Old names for her were *Silver Lady* and *Lady of the Stream*, so I'm not on my own.'

We fished happily away until the fateful High Noon. I took three grayling and John took four, all a respectable two to three pounds. All went back unharmed.

The slanting October sun, the green-red-and-gold dappling of the trees, the autumn smells of the river, the glint and sparkle of the swift run we were fishing, all complemented the

75

beauty of the fish we were taking out. It was one of those mornings you remember forever.

'That was magic, John, the whole thing,' I said back at the Tadchester Arms. 'You were right, you know. There *is* more to fishing than catching fish.'

'Aye,' said John, blowing the froth off his pint. 'I think this is where we came in ...'

CHAPTER 9

Tooth for a Tooth

'If it's not one bloody thing,' said John Denton, 'it's another.'

'I couldn't agree more, John,' I said. 'But go on.'

'Bloody poachers, bloody pollution, bloody pesticides, bloody swans. And now bloody silage.'

We were in the Tadchester Arms, putting back a bit of what the day had taken out. I was taking it steadily, sipping at my Dubonnet and lemonade. John was whopping back the pints of bitter and whisky chasers as if he'd had a hotline call about the imminent end of the world.

'Have another,' he said.

'No thanks, John. I'm not officially on call tonight, but there's bound to be some old love who thinks I'm the only answer to her problems. I was out again this morning at three o'clock. Didn't get back till five. A surgery at eight. Thank God I can't climb trees: they'd be calling me instead of the fire brigade next time a cat goes missing.'

'Too bloody soft, that's your trouble.'

'Soft? That's a hard word, John. Compassion, it's known as in the trade. Caring. Being worried about somebody old, tired and confused. Older, tireder and more confused than I am. That's all it boils down to.'

'Daft I call it.'

'Be fair, John. Was I daft when I came out to look at your dog Biddy when the poachers kicked and broke her leg? Was I daft when you'd followed up a session on the home brew with a lethal dose of time-expired black pudding and thought you were going to die? Was I daft when...'

'All right,' said John. 'I submit. Best of three falls. Give in. Apart from Biddy, you should have told me to bugger off. People take advantage of your good nature.'

'An occupational hazard. A couple of nights ago, in the Gents of this very pub, I had a pillar of society dropping his trousers and begging me to look at his piles. I pleaded bad light and asked him to call in the surgery the next day. I may be soft, John, but what can you do without insulting people or leaving them fretting unnecessarily?'

'You're right lad,' said John. 'So I won't burden you with my troubles. I'm killing the pain, that's all. Wouldn't want to inflict it on anybody else ...'

He stared moodily into his pint pot.

'Come on then, you silly old sod. What's up?'

'No,' said John firmly. 'I couldn't.'

He caught the barmaid's eye, never an easy feat in the Tadchester Arms, but trickier when she was picking her nose.

'Another pint please, love, when you've finished the excavations. Any road ...'

John Denton was the water bailiff on the River Tad. He came as a bit of a shock to upmarket game fishers, down for the weekend, who expected to hear a soft Somerset burr and see a knuckle to the forehead as a sign of respect. What they heard were some flat northcountry vowels and a spade being called a bloody shovel. John's forthright manner and blunt Mancunian speech didn't endear him to some of the snootier elements in Tadchester, but he was a dedicated and highly respected bailiff, especially good at teaching young anglers respect for the water and the wildlife in and around it.

'I've had a bellyful lately,' said John, picking up his pint

78

from the wet patch caused when the barmaid slammed it down on the bar. 'It's a wonder there are any fish left in that river.'

'Poachers again, John?'

'Up to a point. I've cracked most of the organised poaching now with this walkie-talkie.' He pulled a little two-way radio from his pocket. 'I've given up tackling poachers on my own since they did for me and Nellie.' (Both John and his dog had been badly knocked about by a gang several years before). 'So now if I spot 'em, I radio back to Tadchester nick and guide the coppers to the spot. Yes, it's worked well. But there was one bugger I didn't spot the other week and he was using Cymag.'

'I've heard of that somewhere.'

'Quite common around here. Agricultural poison. Cyanide based. Destroys the oxygen in the water. Brings the old salmon up like nothing else. Quieter than gelignite and doesn't blow 'em into fish fingers. But when the poacher's cleared off, the poison's still in the river, floating downstream and killing everything in its path until it gets diluted enough to be harmless. There's a stretch of the Tad now with not a living thing in it. Breaks your heart.'

He took a swig of his pint and a deep breath before starting again.

'As if I hadn't got enough trouble with pollution already. We've had untreated sewage, factory outfall, seepage from the old colliery workings, pesticides from the fields – and now, on top of everything else, there's bloody silage.'

'Silage?'

'Aye. Would you credit it?'

'Surely that's only cattle feed, John?'

'That's right. Green stuff. Grass and kale and the like, fermented in pits and silos with crude molasses. Sounds harmless enough, but the Water Authority boffins tracked down a leakage from that bloody prairie farm – the one where they dug up the hedgerows a few years back – that had seen off some prime fish. Even worse, it was getting into the side streams where the salmon and trout go to spawn. So it not only killed off adult fish, it saw off the whole next generation. What with one thing and another, it's a wonder there's anything left in that river at all.'

'You mentioned swans, John. What's the problem with them?'

'Aye, the swans. The population's right down, and anglers are being blamed for leaving lead shot in the water. I don't deny that happens, nor that some of the swans have gone down with lead poisoning, though I do my best to educate anglers not to leave the stuff about. A couple of the swans have been found dead with spinners down their gullets, too. They'd broken off on snags and the swans had swallowed them. There's not a lot you can do when a swan's swallowed a spinner with a bloody great treble hook on the end.

'But I'm not letting anglers take all the blame. There's more lead gets in the water from the shooting syndicates than from anglers – you should see the pellets spattering down when the shortsighted old buggers blast away at birds near the water. It's a wonder we haven't had fishermen carted off with perforated arses.

'And I'm sure it's not just lead. Apart from pesticides and such in the water, look at the oil and diesel fuel on the surface after the pleasure boats have been charging up and down. The swans are swallowing that day in, day out. Not to mention their nesting being disturbed by all the river traffic.

'And the farmers are glad to have anglers blamed. Smoke screen. Takes the attention off them.'

'What have the farmers got to do with it?'

'Egg-pricking. That's what they've been up to. The swans are partial to young green stuff, and they've learned there's rich pickings away from the water in those kale fields. The farmers daren't shoot the swans, but it doesn't stop them pricking the eggs on the nest. I've found half a dozen nests with the eggs cold and rotten, and each egg with a tiny hole in it. I can't prove anything until I catch somebody at it, but those holes didn't get there on their own. Bloody farmers. Another pint please, love, when you're ready. Christ! She's picking her nose again! Bloody ... '

Another of John's problems was an outbreak of thefts of nightfishers' tackle. Drug-taking and glue-sniffing had finally come to Tadchester and Winchcombe, and gangs of junkies had taken to roaming the river at night, beating up or trussing up anglers, stealing their tackle, and selling it for a few pounds to pay for their next fix.

After one particularly horrific incident, John was forced to ban nightfishing altogether for the anglers' own sakes.

It was 2.30 in the morning when my phone rang.

'Sorry to get you up, Bob,' said John. 'I'm in the phone box by the bridge. Got a patient for you. Casualty. Lost a few teeth and bleeding a lot. Can I bring him over?'

'All right, John. As it's you. Too bloody soft, that's my trouble.'

'Sorry about that, Bob. I'll be there in five minutes.'

The Land Rover pulled up outside. I opened the door to find John helping out a shivering, middle-aged man with a blood-soaked handkerchief clamped over his mouth. When I got him into the light of the surgery, I could see that he was also badly bruised about the face.

I checked to make sure there were no bones broken and then said, 'Right. So far, so good. Let's look at your mouth.'

He took away the handkerchief and opened his mouth with a wince of pain. What I saw was horrifying.

Four or five of his teeth were missing, wrenched out as if some drunken dentist had gone berserk, leaving here and there bits of shattered stump and torn and bleeding gums.

'My God!' I said. 'Who did this?'

'Glue-sniffers or some such,' said John. 'This is Charlie Green, by the way, old mate of mine. They tried to nick Charlie's tackle and he made the mistake of having a go. They knocked him out and cleared off with the lot.

'I found Charlie spark out on the bank, with his tackle missing. All except a pair of pliers the buggers had found in his tackle box. They were on his chest along with bits of teeth. While he was unconscious they'd pulled his bloody teeth out.'

I gave Charlie a couple of local injections and cleaned up the

mess inside his mouth as best I could. The rest of the job would have to be done by a dentist.

'He can stay the night with me,' said John. 'I'll take him round to the dentist in the morning. I tell you one thing, though: I'm going to keep a sharp eye out tomorrow for anybody trying to flog fishing tackle in the town. And if I do find anybody, I'll put some extra business your way. There'll be a few more teeth flying around Tadchester ...'

I crawled back into bed, trying not to disturb Pam, who was just drifting back to sleep.

'You're getting too old for this kind of thing, Bob,' she murmured drowsily. 'What is it this time?'

'John Denton with somebody he found hurt on the bank,' I said.

'Oh dear. I hope he wasn't too bad. But I'd give my eye teeth for you not to be woken up like this.'

'That's nice of you, love,' I said. 'But poor Charlie Green's beaten you to it ...'

CHAPTER 10

Unquenchable Thirsts

One of the early signs of sugar diabetes is an unquenchable thirst. I have had patients coming in to see me in the early stages of diabetes reporting they had been so thirsty that they had even drunk the contents of their hot water bottles during the night. The trouble is that so many of my friends seem to have unquenchable thirsts that sometimes it is difficult not to think of them all as potential diabetics.

The thirstiest of my friends without any doubt was Chris Parfitt, known to everyone as C.P., Editor of the *Tadchester Gazette*, who had the journalist's occupational taste for a pint of beer or three, and he was a connoisseur of its finer points. He and his wife Joyce once disappeared for a week and when they came back he was full of enthusiasm.

'Sorry I didn't let you know about my sudden disappearance,' he said, 'but I didn't want to let anyone know. I'm not desperately sure about the future of the *Tadchester Gazette* so we thought we'd go up north and have a look around. We've been exploring the Pennines. I reckon if I sell my house here and buy a similar house up there for much less money, with a bit of freelancing I could make a reasonable living.'

'And there's another attraction. You'll hardly believe this,'

he said, and his eyes lit up like a man who has just stumbled across the Holy Grail. 'Do you know that up there, a pint of Barnsley Best from the wood, in good condition, costs less than two-thirds the price of an indifferent pint down here?'

'Good God,' I said, 'then I shall have to abandon my practice in Tadchester and look for one in the Pennines.'

Five or six years earlier C.P. had had an operation to restore the power of his voice damaged in a previous throat operation when a nerve was severed and his left vocal cord paralysed. The voice was restored by the injection of Teflon suspension into the paralysed vocal cord which brought the cord back to the midline and stopped the air escaping.

It was a simple but delicate operation and was carried out in Liverpool where the technique, pioneered in the States, was first being carried out in Britain.

C.P. always remembered the day he arrived in hospital,

December 9th, 1980, the day after John Lennon was murdered in New York.

'I thought there'd been a mass local disaster, plane crash or something,' said C.P. 'Nurses, sisters, even matrons were walking about white-faced and sniffling or with tears rolling down their cheeks. All the outpatients looked as if they had had a family bereavement. It wasn't until I went into the TV lounge that I heard the news that John Lennon had been shot. It shook me. I had always been a fan of his but what it did to those Liverpudlian girls who had grown up with the Beatles as their local heroes, was cataclysmic. From the look of them the whole city must have been in mourning.'

The operation was a complete success but C.P. was lucky to come home alive. Though his stay at hospital was short, it was fraught with temptation. The window of his ward overlooked a little pub on the other side of the main road. Lunchtime and evening he watched with growing frustration, the locals walking to the pub and reeling out happily two or three hours later. Before his operation he was on a no-liquids diet which made his torment even worse. After the operation he was to have neither food nor drink for a while.

'I felt great after the operation Bob,' he said. 'It was done under a local anaesthetic so I had no after effects at all and I could have murdered a pint. I thought the no-liquids rule was just a bit of hospital bureaucracy – you know, like waking you up to give you a sleeping pill. In the end I decided to throw a few clothes on and sneak out for a swift one, but I couldn't find my clothes. They had been moved to a cupboard in the sister's office.'

'Perhaps to keep them safe while you were out of the ward,' I said. 'Or perhaps they didn't want to lose a patient after all the trouble they'd gone to.'

'Why? One pint couldn't have done me any harm.'

'It could have drowned you.'

'Get away.'

'I'm serious,' I said. 'The local anaesthetic would have paralysed your epiglottis, leaving you no control over your swallowing until it wore off. If you had swigged a pint it would have gone straight into your lungs.'

'By heck!' said C.P. 'What a story – Patient Dies in Mercy Dash–Dry Land Drowning Drama!'

'Front page news if ever there was,' I said. 'But you wouldn't have been around to write it.'

'That's true,' said C.P. 'No use going to all that bother if somebody else was going to get the byline.'

The pub was the first place C.P. made for on his discharge. Not only did he fancy a pint, he also had a morbid fear and dislike of hospitals. He had bad memories of when, as a child, he had contracted mumps and scarlet fever and had spent a month in a hospital where the food was atrocious. The memory had lingered on.

C.P. was driving back from Liverpool by car so he stuck to the limit of two pints, not enough to get the flavour of the place. But he had to go back to Liverpool at intervals of two or three months for check-ups and then he made sure he went by train. His check-ups generally took place around noon, leaving him plenty of time for a lunchtime pint afterwards.

After one examination, which confirmed that all was well, C.P. nipped over the road for his customary swig of local atmosphere. There he found himself a charitable mission which gave his visits to the pub even more of a point. Towards closing time, as the landlady was poised to ring the bell, C.P. glanced at the door and noticed a man across the road halted by the traffic lights. A big man in a donkey jacket, he had one leg in plaster up to the thigh, was balancing on a crutch, and was waving another in the air, shouting hoarsely in the direction of the pub.

C.P. could not make out what the man was shouting because of the din of the traffic, but he recognised the gestures of desperation.

'Could you hold the bell please, love?' he asked the landlady. 'Disabled customer in distress on his way over.'

The landlady stayed her hand, the traffic lights changed and the big man made record time across the road in the

Multiple Fracture, Full-Length Cast and Two Crutches Handicap Sprint.

'Bless you, pal,' the man gasped as he crashed through the doorway. 'Saved my life. Pint of bitter please, love.'

On his next visit C.P. made it his business to look across the road towards closing time. Sure enough there was another thirsty outpatient trapped by the lights.

'Hold it please, love,' he said again, and another distressed customer's life was saved.

He got his reward a couple of visits later when his examination was deferred until the early afternoon. Still living in hopes of a pint later he was dismayed to find the consulting room packed with medical students, all of whom were there to have a look at the successful result of his operation. One by one the students peered down his throat through an orinascope. It was a lengthy process, with the consultant holding down C.P.'s tongue with a spatula. It was a ticklish process too, which caused C.P. now and again to gag on the spatula and hold things up further still. As the last student finished, C.P. glanced at his watch. Two-forty, only twenty minutes to get out and across the road for a flying pint. Still, it was all over now.

'Thank you gentlemen,' said the consultant. 'A very successful operation as you've seen for yourselves. Everybody *was* able to see it I take it?'

The students nodded and murmured assent, except for one student from Hong Kong at the back of the group.

'Sorry,' he said. 'Many apologies. I did not see very well at all.'

'In that case, you had better take another look,' said the consultant.

C.P. prided himself on his complete lack of racial prejudice. But with dreams of a pint evaporating before his eyes, he allowed himself just one lapse.

'Chinese twit!' he hissed.

It was all over in a few minutes, but to C.P. it seemed to take hours. He thanked the consultant, made hurried farewells to the room, scuttled to the reception desk to get the date for his

87

next appointment, then flew down the stairs and out of the hospital. The traffic lights were against him and it was now two minutes to three.

'Hold it!' he yelled, hopping up and down waving his arms towards the pub door.

After an eternity the lights turned green and he was off from a standing start that would have left Zola Budd still on the starting blocks. He fell through the pub door just as the bell for time gave a brassy and unfeeling clang.

'Sod it!' he wailed.

'It's all right, love,' said the landlady placing a foaming pint of bitter on the bar. 'We saw you coming.'

'You're an angel,' said C.P. taking a long swig and fishing for his money.

'Paid for,' said the landlady. 'Chap by the door.'

The big man by the door raised his pint.

'All the best, Whack,' he said. 'Good health.'

'What do I owe you?' said C.P.

'Nothing,' said the big man. 'You saved me life once, remember?'

C.P. thought for a second. 'Oh yes,' he said 'it all comes back to me now. I didn't recognise you without your leg in plaster.'

*   *   *

I thought it would be sensible to test C.P.'s urine just in case he had developed a tendency to diabetes, a condition his grandmother and a couple of aunts had suffered from. (It is family and friends who get least noticed when they are ill. Gladys had once said that if she had walked into the surgery with an arrow through her head, nobody would have asked her what was wrong with her).

I gave C.P. a little stick, a clinistic. This has two little coloured plaques which give clear indications of whether there is any sugar in the water. If there is, the little blue patch on the stick will turn to brown.

'Come on,' I said to C.P. in the Tadchester Arms one evening. 'There's no time like the present. Go and wee on your stick.'

He went off the the Gents and returned in a few minutes looking a bit shamefaced and handed me back the little stick. The portion of the stick with the indicators on was completely burnt away.

'Good God!' I said. 'This is a new one on me. You've made medical history. What have you been drinking – firewater?'

'Sorry Bob,' said C.P. 'My mistake. I had the thing in my hand as I went out and I accidentally tamped my pipe with it. Give us another stick and I'll have another go.'

I produced another stick which C.P. was careful not to set fire to. Happily, the indicator showed he was clear. I raised my glass.

'Here's a toast to prolonged good health and this move to the Pennines,' I said. 'Just think, C.P., if Barnsley Best is as cheap as that, you could afford to have a bath in the stuff.'

C.P.'s eyes lit up for a second, then a look of horror crept in. 'Bath in it? he said. 'In Barnsley Best? Good God, Bob – have you no *respect*?'

CHAPTER 11

Sabbatical Leave

It had been decided in the practice that we each in turn, once every seven years, should have a three-month sabbatical holiday. The idea had been sprung from a couple of five-week Saharan trips I made when my ever-patient partners had allowed me to pay for a locum. Paying for a locum sounds like a luxury – and so it was – but I had earned some money from writing.

One expedition had been as a paying member on a 4,000-mile circuit through Algeria, Niger, up to the Tassili Plateau in Niger to look at rock and cave drawings. I went again as a paid medical officer for the same company, escorting some rich but delightful Americans along the same route.

The first to go on his sabbatical was Steve Maxwell our senior partner who went to Nepal for three months. He spent two months working in a mission hospital, then a month exploring some remoter parts of Nepal. Being Steve, he hardly mentioned it when he came back. It was very difficult to wheedle out of him what had happened, but he had seen a whole array of medical cases: diseases like tuberculosis which have almost disappeared from Britain, but which are still rife in Nepal. There was one small change when he came back. At the reception hatch there was a collection tin towards a new roof for the mission hospital he had worked in.

Henry Johnson's sabbatical was in Kenya. He had relatives there and some connection with the flying doctor service. He balanced his sabbatical with a more normal holiday, spending half his time sunbathing in Mombasa and in safari parks, and the other half flying around doing emergency surgery in the remotest parts.

Jack Hart's sabbatical was the simplest of all. He and his wife Joan just went to Southern Italy and lay in the sun for three months, coming back with absolutely the darkest sunburns that we had ever seen.

My sabbatical came about six months after Pam's hip operation and eighteen months after my coronary bypass. We decided to use it to continue our love affair with France and really to get progressively fit and well.

One of the problems of general practice is that you never seem to have enough time to enjoy the place where you live, and we were determined to spend some time doing that. But to make symbolically sure that we were starting doing something different, we booked a three-day holiday in Boulogne at the beginning of our three months off.

We went by boat-train. Having travelled many times on spruce inter-city trains to London, we were surprised at the shabby boat train down to Folkestone. But Boulogne was a lovely city and we had a good hotel. We did a lot of walking. The market was colourful, food inexpensive, the cathedral on top of the hill a good test for both my heart and Pam's hip. The only things that marred the trip were the eternal busloads of our fellow countrymen arriving on day trips, principally to go shopping in the supermarket.

I'm sure that the vast majority behaved themselves. Crocodiles of English schoolchildren with harassed-looking teachers wound their way demurely around most of the major sights. But wandering down the main streets and in the restaurants where we ate were ill-behaved louts, at twelve noon already much the worse for drink, supporting inebriated and almost

91

unconscious girls. Half a dozen young Britishers made awful scenes, then staggered off to the supermarket which, when we visited it in the afternoon, was again full of our countrymen buying vast amounts of liquor to take back home. Many were behaving very badly and buying such quantities of alcohol – trays and trays of beer – quite beyond their ability to carry. I am sure these were the unrepresentative few, but I certainly wasn't proud of being British.

After a spell at home again we set off for a long holiday in France, crossing this time by the Dover-to-Calais route. Again, the train and boat were dirty and the crews sloppy. Things could have been better.

This planned holiday was an exciting one. We were to travel by sleeper on the famous Blue Train to the South of France and stay in Carnon in the Camargue about six miles west of the great French resort of La Grande Motte which is characterised by its spectacular and well-planned modern buildings. We had a compartment to ourselves with two bunks, toilet and wash-basin. A hot meal with some wine was served to us: it was a home of our own, a genuine wagonlit. The only difficulty was trying to sleep with the train going at 150 miles an hour, swaying and banging along the tracks and occasionally stopping at stations.

The final destination of the train was Menton, by the border with Italy, but we got off at Arles, the lovely old Roman town that used to be the capital of the Languedoc area.

After breakfast in the local restaurant we were taken by coach to Carnon. As we drove through the Camargue I saw for the first time wind-ruffled fields of rice, flamingos wading in pink flocks, the famous white horses splashing through the water. There were great shallow lakes on one side, the Canal du Midi following the road for much of the way, and the sea on the other side. There was an incredible feeling of space and suddenly we passed acres and acres of close-planted vines. The single biggest vineyard in France is in this area. We visited it on one of our day trips. In the height of the picking season 10,000 tons of grapes, most of which are picked by machine, are crushed to be made into wine. The machines spoiled my romantic images of grape picking, and the wine they offered us for tasting spoiled any thought we had of buying wine from this particular vineyard.

Carnon is little more than a new marina with shops, restaurants and apartments shooting up all over the place. It had been beautifully planned so that our main hotel room was only about 20 yards from the harbour and we could sit and watch people messing about with boats. I don't know how many serious sailors there were there; it seemed much more important to the owners that the boats were polished and shining and well provided with food and drink, rather than they should be sailed.

We explored many of the areas and towns round about. Montpellier is a lovely old town, with one of France's oldest if not most important medical schools. As we sat down for lunch in a restaurant the man next to us spoke to his companion in perfect English. The conversation was about the various aspects of sputum. It all sounded vaguely familiar but it didn't go too well with the food. They were two physicians from Barts Hospital in London, who were on some course at Montpellier. They were moved on to another table, as ours could accommodate four more people, and the food tasted much better after that.

Montpellier was a lovely old town with views from avenues of trees leading to a monument at the end of the town. To my surprise, as in many other French towns, there were a number of beggars.

To show how fit we were we walked seven miles to Las Pavalos, the next port along the coast, and back.

Another magical place we visited was Sete. It was almost another Venice, interlaced with rivers and canals. The town was obstructed by public works. The canal in one area of the town was blocked off to build an underground car park. It seemed funny parking under water.

We had a day going through the Camargue by boat seeing much of the wild life: the bulls of the Camargue, the white horses, the flamingos and a host of other birds. It was all over too quickly and before we knew where we were, we were standing on the station at Arles being stung unmercifully by mosquitoes, waiting for our wagon-lit to take us back to England.

The next part of our holiday, back in England, was concentrated on our other love: the Thames. With our friends Joe and Lynne Church, we were hiring a boat from Wallingford, Oxfordshire, down to Chertsey in Surrey, then along the riverway and canals up to Guildford.

The river was running very high when we picked up our boat and it was raining heavily. The first lock keeper thought the whole thing would be over by the weekend, so we pushed on through the most glorious countryside to Goring and Streatley and moored near the Child Beale Trust on the stretch of river running up to Pangbourne.

It was strange at night, lying in the boat and hearing cries of the various birds from this Trust, set up by an old gentleman, for children. With the noise of hundreds of different birds, many of them protected, it was like being in the African jungle.

Next day it was still raining and the river was still rising, we debated all day whether to go on, as there was a big weir to negotiate at Pangbourne. Things appeared a little better in the afternoon so we set off, negotiated the lock comfortably, and made for the next stretch.

Our next lock was at Mapledurham. There we found the whole lock under water, with men in red armbands directing the traffic.

'Head into the weir stream as you go out of the lock,' said one of the officials. 'Otherwise the current will take you into the bank.'

We did as he instructed, headed into the weir stream, and bobbed around like a cork. It was all very exciting although my crew were looking a bit apprehensive. We bowled along with the current down safely through Caversham Lock in Reading, then even faster still towards Sonning Lock. It was still raining and the river was still rising. When we arrived at Sonning Lock we asked for some advice about where to moor.

'You're better mooring above the lock,' said the lock keeper, 'it's a bit rough down below. The water is still rising. But now you are here, go through the bridge and then try to moor in the bank. Get in behind some trees or any other shelter.'

It was a sad relection on our times that there was a large warning notice on Sonning Lock saying 'Beware of Vandals who Jump on the Boat as You Go Through Sonning Bridge'. It was unlikely that we would have trouble today, but Joe and I had a couple of mooring stakes handy to repel boarders. Who would ever have imagined piracy on the River Thames?

Going through the weir stream before Sonning Lock was much like our experiences at Mapledurham. The River Thames was showing how strong it could be and we were thankful to get out of the turbulent waters. We looked for a spot to pull into the bank and moor safely for the night. We spotted a likely place and went about a hundred yards past to see if there was a better one and then turned round and went back upstream with the throttle full open. There was a great bow wave and when I looked at the bank I realised we weren't moving forward. The hundred yards to get back to the secluded mooring spot took us three-quarters of an hour. We obviously weren't going to go anywhere until the Thames settled down.

We tied the boat up with about five lots of lines and were stuck there for three days. Occasionally boats would move past us but they were much more powerful than ours. We saw hired boats going up in convoy, often being pulled by tugs.

Sonning Lock was our nearest water supply and as we were running short of water, it meant repeated journeys to and fro with our two gallon can. After three days we rang home to tell them that we were all right, to find that they had desperately been trying to get in touch with us. The bad news was that my elder son Trevor, who had been filming on Sark, had fallen and broken his hip, and was now in hospital in Guernsey. Could we get over there as soon as possible?

We set off in the turbulent stream down to the next lock,

Shiplake Lock. We just managed to get into the boatyard below the lock. Then we took a taxi back to Wallingford and explained our problem at the Wallingford Travel Agency.

They couldn't have been more helpful. The local manager was being visited by the area manager, who had a friend in Guernsey who ran the Old Government House Hotel. He rang him and booked us in, then booked us a plane and a car to meet us at Guernsey Airport. From calling at the Wallingford travel agency at 11 a.m., we were in Guernsey by six o'clock that evening. Back on the Thames, our boat was later picked up by some friends who lived in the Berkshire village of Woolhampton, Bernard and Joyce Walter. They brought it back to Wallingford when the floods had subsided.

In Guernsey we drove straight to the hospital. We found Trevor just coming round from his anaesthetic. Although his hip had been pinned by a urologist, it had been done expertly. It was a great relief to see him.

He had been acting in a television series, *Mr Pye*, for Channel Four, and this would have been his last day on the island. Taking a short cut, he had come to a sunken roadway. The bank had given way and Trevor fell almost in front of an oncoming tractor.

The crew sent for the doctor who came on his bicycle – cars aren't allowed on Sark – and for the ambulance, which is a caravan pulled by a tractor. Then via the hospital boat, the *Flying Christine*, he was whipped across the water to Guernsey to the Princess Elizabeth Hospital.

The hospital really was first class. They seemed to have many more nurses than we do in England. I think the National Health Service has a lot to learn from Guernsey; there always seemed to be somebody about and the nursing care was absolutely excellent.

Trevor's hospital stay cost him nothing; as a British National he was covered by a reciprocal arrangement with the NHS. This is not the same for Guernsey people. It costs them £10 every time they visit their general practitioner, £90 a day if they are in hospital. I felt certain that my appoint-

ment list would shorten at home if everybody was charged £10 a time.

We spent two weeks in Guernsey exploring the island, visiting Trevor every day until he was well enough to come home by plane.

The Old Government House Hotel took one back thirty years. The accommodation and food were superb. There were no extras. You still left your shoes outside your room to be cleaned at night. Instead of getting fit and lean on the river, I got fatter and fatter on the food of Guernsey.

They could only put us up for a couple of days at the Government House Hotel, but the manager booked us into a country club where again we were treated with the utmost kindness.

Trevor was checked by one of my orthopaedic consultant friends when we got back home and it was pronounced that a perfect job had been done on Guernsey.

The end of our sabbatical was drawing to a close. As a finale we had five days by car in Normandy and Brittany with two friends, Des and Joan. We travelled from Portsmouth to Cherbourg on a Townsend Thoreson boat which was a complete contrast to the boats on which we had crossed before. This boat was immaculate. Even the people who were cleaning the floors and clearing the tables had spotless linen coats and trousers on. The restaurants were immaculate, the food was absolutely first class, and there was plenty of room and accommodation.

We spent our first night at Barfleur, the little port on the top of the Cherbourg peninsula from where William the Conqueror set sail for England. We travelled down to see the Bayeux Tapestry, on for a couple of nights in Dinan, a fascinating town with a huge castle wall overlooking the River Rance. We had a marvellous meal in a restaurant where the madame seemed to cook, do the bills, the wine, everything. Its popularity was confirmed by the queue of people outside.

Our last two days were spent in Dinard, the seaside resort. We went round looking at properties, we always do, I cannot think of holidays when we haven't said, 'We must come back and get an apartment here.' Perhaps, who knows, one day we will.

A trip back on the Townsend Thoreson ferry, and our sabbatical was over. We had crammed a lot into it, three trips to France, our abortive river trip and a fortnight in Guernsey. I was quite exhausted.

When I went back to the surgery I felt I had been away a hundred years.

'A good sabbatical?' said Steve. 'How are you feeling?'

'To be quite honest,' I said, 'I feel just like a holiday to get over it all.'

*   *   *

I wasn't the only one to benefit from a sabbatical that year.

Chris Parfitt, the man with a fondness for Barnsley Best, came into the surgery one day with his symptoms typed out on a piece of paper.

'Don't want to waste your time, Bob,' he said. 'And it saves me forgetting anything.'

The paper read:

98

'For the past few weeks I've been waking up in the middle of the night for no apparent reason. My heart has been working faster than usual, and I've had this strange feeling of fear.

'Once I'm awake, I start fretting about all sorts of things, mainly the future: how the wife and I will survive on my measly pension after my retirement from the *Gazette*; whether the kids (he had two grown-up children, both living and working away from home) will survive the pressures on them and live happy and fulfilled lives; whether I ought to get the chimney stack re-pointed before the thing falls through the roof; whether that stain on the garage beams really is the start of dry rot – all sorts of silly things which normally I'd dismiss or do something about.

'Last night I was sitting in the Tadchester Arms, enjoying a quiet pint and quite relaxed, as I thought, when all of a sudden my heart started pumping. It was going so fast I thought something was going to blow. I left the pub and, during the walk home, had to make a conscious effort, by deep breathing and what willpower I could summon, to get my heart back to something like a normal beat.

'Even so, I woke up during the night with the damn thing racing and all the fears crowding in again. In a word, Bob – *HELP!*'

'I think you've diagnosed yourself here, C.P.,' I said. 'Sounds like stress if anything did.'

'But I've nothing to be stressed about. I'm on top of my job, the kids are off our hands and the bank has stopped sending me threatening letters. Where's the stress?'

'Don't forget you've been living on adrenalin all your life,' I said. 'You're meeting deadlines all the time and the old fight-or-flight mechanism is what gives you the speed to meet them. You're not switching off. And you do tend to burn the candle at both ends, old lad.'

C.P., as I have already related, liked his ale and enjoyed the company in the local pubs. He also hated inactivity. The days were too short for him and he'd sit up into the small hours, talking or reading, and be up early the following morning.

Nor was his job either a routine or peaceful one. Jackson Wilder, the hardnosed and tight-fisted proprietor of the *Gazette*, made sure he got his money's worth.

I sounded C.P.'s heart, which seemed strong enough; checked his pulse, which was too fast for my liking; and took his blood pressure, which was high.

'What you could do with,' I said, writing out a prescription for beta-blockers which would inhibit the flow of adrenalin, 'is a good long holiday with plenty of fresh air and exercise. Get yourself away from that desk and the telephone for a while. A sabbatical wouldn't come amiss; I've just had one myself and I can thoroughly recommend it.'

'Great, Bob,' he said. 'I'll try for one.'

He was back the following week for a blood pressure check, looking very down.

'That miserable old bugger Wilder says that no way is he letting me go gallivanting in the firm's time and on his money,' he said. 'If I want time out of the office I've got to justify it by producing some copy for the paper. A right busman's holiday that'd be.'

But he was back the following week, waving a copy of the *Gazette*.

'I've cracked it, Bob,' he said, pointing to a front page story. 'That's me – the *Gazette*'s Man of the Woods!'

There was a picture of C.P. looking ridiculous in a camouflage jacket and a Davy Crockett hat, brandishing a large axe and grinning menacingly at a tree.

'For God's sake, C.P.!' I said. 'When I said exercise I meant walking or digging the garden. You'll kill yourself waving that thing about!'

'That's only for the picture,' said C.P. 'And I wouldn't be seen dead with that former cat on my head. Just read the story.'

The story was about a group of conservation-minded Tadchester citizens who had banded together to take over Downhanger Wood, a large tract of beech and oak which had been allowed to run wild by absentee owners. Calling themselves The Men of the Woods, they had bought the land through public subscription and were now proposing to clear the dead and diseased trees and hack away the tangled under-growth which was choking the place. They were appealing to local businessmen for funds and for volunteers to do the unskilled clearing work.

'They tapped up old Wilder for a subscription,' said C.P. 'He went white. Blood from a stone has nothing on getting him to part with his money. And that's where I saw my chance.

'"Give them publicity," I said to Wilder. "That'd be worth more to them than cash." And I offered to write a big feature every week for a month on the clearance operation, provided I could work in the woods myself as a volunteer. I'd be getting my sabbatical for the price of a couple of hours' writing a week and Wilder would get plenty of column inches for the *Gazette*. He'd save his cash, he'd get lots of public prestige from campaigning features about Saving our Heritage and – this is what clinched it – he could approach all the local firms spon-soring the operation to place ads with the *Gazette*. Even he saw that he couldn't lose on the deal – so I start on Monday as your friendly neighbourhood Man of the Woods.'

'Sounds OK,' I said. 'So long as you don't overdo it. What exactly is involved?'

'No axe work, for a start,' said C.P. 'Felling of the big trees is being done by paid professionals with chainsaws. I'm cutting down or pulling up all the sycamore and maple saplings which are infesting the wood and crowding out the native beech and oak. I'm using heavy duty secateurs and a log saw to cut them down, then painting the stumps with herbicide to stop them sprouting up again. While I'm in the woods, I'm also supposed to stop motorcyclists using the place for scramble practice, but I think I'll give that a miss: I've grown attached to my front teeth.'

Off he went, singing *I'm a lumberjack and I'm OK*, and that was the last I saw of him for four weeks, though I followed his pro-gress in the *Gazette* and gathered from his articles that forestry work wasn't quite the idyllic pursuit he'd expected it to be.

On the last Saturday of his stint he called in for a check-up and a repeat prescription of the tablets. 'Called in' is perhaps not the best description. 'Crawled in' would be nearer the mark. Though he looked weatherbeaten, it would be incorrect to say he looked fit. He was limping, was bent forward from the waist in a Max Wall crouch, and blew his nose loudly every couple of minutes.

'How are you, then?' I asked.

'Knackered,' wheezed C.P.

'Yerss ... I have seen you looking more sprightly. Let's try the old blood pressure, shall we?'

His blood pressure was well down, still on the high side but a lot better than it was.

'Your sabbatical seems to have done the trick,' I said.

'It's bloody near done for me,' he croaked, and broke into a coughing fit.

'Not what you expected, I gather?'

'Not a bit. You can stick forestry work from now on. Give me a month in the abbatoir any time.'

'What was the problem?'

'What *wasn't* the problem? Aaaah – CHOO! Excuse me.

'First of all, I'd never appreciated the size of these woods. Probably because I'd never tried to hack my way through them before. And I'd never realised there were so many sycamores in the world. Millions of 'em, springing up like bamboo. A dog couldn't get through some of those thickets. I was shifting up to a thousand a day of the smaller saplings, sometimes more, and still only clearing a patch the size of a backyard.

'I used the saw to cut down the bigger ones, and to avoid leaving a tall stump I had to crouch and saw close to the ground. That did my back a lot of good, I can tell you.

'And wet! There is nothing wetter or colder than a wood first thing in the morning. On the first day I got soaked to the skin, so I bought myself a rubberised fisherman's outfit. I only used it twice, though. When I got down to the job I worked up such a sweat that I was getting soaked from the inside; my socks were squelching in my wellies. So I went back to getting wet from the outside.

'As the day warmed up, it brought out the midges. I had a bush hat to keep them off my head, but they bit everywhere else they could land on.'

'Still,' I said, 'you did have the consolation of knowing that you were doing a worthwhile job. People round here will be grateful for it.'

'Don't kid yourself,' said C.P. 'The first people I met were two ladies out for a walk. I rose from a thicket just as they were passing, and they ran off screaming. After that I wore a cyclist's fluorescent Sam Browne belt and whistled myself dry so that it wouldn't happen again.

'Another old lady came up to me and said she hoped that I'd tidy the place up after me. Never mind the fact that I was doing it all for nothing. She didn't want her woods – *her* woods! – looking a mess.

'Two yobbos on a motorbike came roaring down a bridle path near where I was working. I raised my hand to stop them and have a few gentle words, but the rider speeded up and skidded passed me, covering me in mud. His pillion rider stood up, gave me a V-sign and yelled things to the effect that I was a silly old pillock.

'Then, to top it all, a bloke came charging down from a big house on the edge of the wood – thinking I was nicking the trees for firewood – and set three bloody dogs on me. Three! If I hadn't got in first with the old power-packed welly I could have been coming here for a wooden leg.

'I gave him a piece of my mind, forgetting that I represented the finest traditions of the *Gazette* – whatever those may be – and he wasn't too pleased. Neither was I when I found out he was a masonic mate of old Wilder.'

'Never mind,' I said. 'There must have been some compensation from all the wildlife you saw while you were working.'

'Wildlife? There was one pigeon which shit on my head when I took my hat off for a scratch, one geriatric squirrel with

a bald tail, a frog which turned up twice, and a dog which cocked its leg over me as I was crouching down.

'Anyway, whatever wildlife is in that wood, I don't think I've done it any favours.'

'Why not?'

'They forgot to mention the bird sanctuary. A local ornithologist had pegged out a particularly overgrown patch to observe the numbers and habits of the birds in a given area of dense growth. By the time I'd stumbled upon the pegs, the place wasn't dense any more: I'd chopped the bloody lot down.'

'Oh dear,' I said. 'I suppose you're glad it's all over. Still, you're all the better for it.'

'I certainly don't feel it. I could do with a holiday to get over it all.'

'Steady on,' I said 'You're pinching my lines ...'

* * *

The sabbatical did do C.P. good, though, despite his moans. Apart from toning him up physically and lowering his blood pressure, it distanced him from his worries and allowed him to get things into perspective. He lived in a big old house with a fair bit of land, and its value had appreciated considerably over the years. On his retirement he could sell up, move into a smaller place, and have a decent sum to invest to supplement his pension. (As his wife, Joyce, said, if he'd gone on worrying about his pension, he wouldn't be around to collect it.) He realised too, that he could supplement his income in his retirement by writing the odd freelance article: his skills were portable, so it didn't really matter where he lived. Perhaps he would make it to the Pennines yet!

He had the chimney stack pointed and the garage timbers treated; two more worries less. And when his married son told him that he was shortly to become a grandfather, C.P. was left without a worry in the world.

CHAPTER 12

Auntie Kitty

I first met Pam's aunts, Kitty and Daisy, at our wedding. They were already legends in her family, both in their seventies: two delightful, contented ladies who had lived quiet, genteel lives and of whom I never heard a cross word.

Daisy once had a job of some sort, but Kitty had never gone out to work. She had spent most of what would have been a normal working life looking after her parents. They must have been of reasonably affluent means, as between the wars they regularly went abroad for their holidays. They were not rich, but they were obviously very comfortably off.

Daisy died when she was about eighty, leaving Kitty on her own in the family house they had shared. Though she now had only herself to look after, Kitty kept busy. She gave freely of her time to such worthy organisations as the local lifeboat fund and horticultural society, of which she was president for many years.

She once came to stay with Gerry, Pam's late father, when he lived in an annex to our house. I cooked a Chinese meal for us all, and Kitty tucked in with relish to these new and strange dishes. She was then in her mid eighties, mobile, active and spry.

We had no more real contact with her until Pam, on a trip up to London, called in to see her. The house that she remembered as a little girl as being grand and imposing was now a crumbling wreck, not so very big after all. Kitty, now in her early nineties, was living in a state of complete confusion.

She insisted on remaining independent, although it must have been a hazard every time she left her house. What had been her front garden had been compulsorily purchased, and what had been a quiet country lane was now a major road.

Finally, at ninety-five, she acknowledged she was no longer fit enough to manage on her own and elected to move into an Eventide Home in North Wembley. She liked it particularly because there was a pond by which she could sit and watch the birds and feed the ducks. It also had nice gardens and she was able to go and give a hand with the blooms. We used to visit her there once or twice a year. We would have tea with her and a little walk in the garden.

She had a hilarious holiday with us when she was about ninety-eight. She couldn't get up the stairs and so I had to carry her up with a fireman's lift on my shoulder. She came downstairs on her own, bumping down on her bottom and shouting, 'Look at my bloomers! I hope they can't see them in the street!'

She enjoyed everything. Her main complaint about the retirement home was that it was full of old people. She played whist regularly twice a week until she was 106. She always remembered her Chinese meal, and Pam's father saying: 'If you'll eat that, you'll eat anything.'

Kitty got progressively frailer and was eventually confined to travelling about in a wheelchair, but she still enjoyed her twice weekly games of whist and any other entertainment or trips put on by the home.

When we went to see her, she would wake up, a little tiny, frail figure on the bed, open her eyes and say, 'Hello, Pam. Hello, Bob,' and then would straightaway drop into conversations about things we had done together, ask questions about the children and reminisce about the Chinese meal. It was as if we'd seen her only the week before.

Her sight was beginning to fail and she was getting a bit arthritic, but her mind stayed clear. She couldn't read very well but she seemed to take memories out like transparencies and have a look and a chuckle at them. She never ever reprimanded us for not visiting her more often. The main load of taking care of her fell on Pam's brother, Theo, who managed all her legal and financial affairs.

She certainly wouldn't part with her money without a struggle. One day she had to have a new pair of glasses and the optician asked, 'Have you got a hundred pounds Miss Baynton?'

'Yes,' said Auntie Kitty, 'but you won't get it from me. Any dealings you have must be with my cousin.' At this stage all men were her cousins.

I used to pull her leg about her age.

'Come on Kitty, tell us about the Relief of Mafeking,' I said once.

'Oh, shut up, Bob,' she said. 'I had a lot of friends in Mafeking.'

Kitty had been born in 1877. She was twenty-three at the turn of the century and thirty-seven when the First World War broke out. At the age of 107, she said to me, 'You know, this Common Market business is sound politically but bad economically.' Who could argue with her, with all her experience?

In her last year, because of her failing sight and increasing arthritis, she was unable for the first time to send out her own Christmas cards. This was a great blow to her.

She died peacefully three weeks before her 108th birthday, a fine, lovely old lady. I never heard her criticise anyone, I never knew her anything but good-natured and entertaining, well informed and highly intellectual. I think that the secret of her great age was the fact that she took everything calmly as it came along. She had been fortunate in that she hadn't been pressed financially, but on the other hand she hadn't squandered her resources; there were still a few pennies left in the bank to go to some South African relative after her death.

I always wondered why she hadn't married. Theo, going through her papers afterwards, found some letters and pictures which gave away part of her secret. She had had a young man when she was in her early twenties and there was a postcard from him: a handsome dark-haired young man, sitting in a Victorian or Edwardian pose at a table, and on the back a note saying, 'I'll see you soon my dear. I'd love to come and bite your nose.' This was obviously some form of secret language between them.

So this was her love, the man to whom she was faithful for the next eighty-five years. He died sometime around about 1900. It was possibly tuberculosis, or he may had died in the South African war. Kitty never talked about him. It was only from the letters and photographs that we learned of the most beautiful, touching and loving relationship she had with the man she intended to marry. There was no trace anywhere of the sadness or bitterness she must have felt when she lost him.

She was lucky that she had found, for a time anyway, her one and only true love. Like all people who are remembered, he never completely died; for Kitty, always something of him remained. She had had this love and part of it had remained alive in her forever. Nothing had spoiled it, she had kept it to herself, hadn't had to share it with anybody, and it had helped to sustain her against all life's harassment.

Although we only saw her rarely, I miss her and I acknowledge that perhaps she had got closer to the real art of knowing how to live than anybody that I've ever met. God bless her.

*   *   *

Nurse Jones did not reach the great heights of Auntie Kitty's age, but did manage to reach a respectable ninety-six. Her life was quite different from Kitty's, and primarily devoted to nursing. There had been a husband some way back, but seemingly no children, and odd relatives somewhere in Kent that she used to visit.

She had been a nurse and midwife in Tadchester, presumably since her early twenties. She knew the inside story of every family in the district, about which she was not always too discreet. She kept on nursing into her nineties when she used to come into infant welfare clinics and help hand out vitamins and medicines. She almost had to be carried there and carried back but it did give her a feeling of some importance.

She lived in a small cluster of houses about two miles out of town which had been specially designed for the retired and elderly. There was one small shop, a garage and a pub there, but – with true forward-thinking municipal planning – there was no public transport.

From about her mid eighties to her death at ninety-six, Nurse Jones' health was indifferent. For the last five or six years it was awful, with repeated chest infections. She would be found by neighbours lying on the floor and I had to send her into hospital many times, always thinking she would not come out. Not that I thought she would die, but I thought that the hospital wouldn't let her return to live on her own.

Very recently arrived in the group of houses – and in Tadchester that meant about five or six years ago – was a lady, a Mrs St Clair. And by a lady I mean a lady.

She had been a companion at one of the big houses nearby and insisted on her independence. She had a furnished apartment which was always immaculate, and a dog, cat and budgerigar for company. She was always doing something: making curtains, gardening, knitting cardigans for somebody's baby, or sewing for the W.I. She was virtually a one-woman social service for the little community. Everybody expected Mrs St Clair to do things for them.

'Mrs St Clair, will you get my prescription?'

'Mrs St Clair, will you do my shopping?'

People visiting sick relatives in this little enclave went away happy with the thought that Mrs St Clair would be keeping an eye on their elderly kinfolk, although in some cases it was the last thing Mrs St Clair wanted to do. She had many interests of her own and hadn't really come here to look after other people, but somehow it became her lot. At Christmas she had about five or six people round to dinner. Nurse Jones always managed to get returned from hospital by declaring that Mrs St Clair would look after her.

Nurse Jones, game that she was, became slightly confused as she got older. She insisted on living alone, despite the great effort it took to reach and answer the front door. She used to go to bed at six o'clock in the evening which meant that she got up at three in the morning. She always used to tell me that I was the best doctor in the world, that she would never manage without me. When I'd gone, she would say the most scurrilous things about me. I was not alone; she said scurrilous things about everybody, especially her home helps, who tended not to stay long.

With one chest infection, she fell out of bed and was found there by Mrs St Clair who from then on, made an early morning visit every day. It reached the stage when Mrs St

111

Clair, apart from all her duties to her other neighbours, was providing all Nurse Jones' meals, tidying her flat and not getting too many thanks for it.

I think that I must have sent Nurse Jones into hospital at least twelve times, when she had become completely unmanageable at home and when it often looked as if she wouldn't last more than a few days. It was grossly unfair that Mrs St Clair should be burdened with Nurse Jones, and for years we tried to persuade her to go somewhere she could be looked after. Eventually after one particularly bad incident in hospital, she agreed to go to a special home for retired nurses.

Mrs St Clair kept in touch with Nurse Jones, visiting her in the home, writing to her and telephoning her regularly. It was she who broke the news to me of a sudden and vast improvement in Nurse Jones' health. What had happened was that this cantankerous and ailing lady of ninety-five had fallen in love. It was with another resident of the home, which must have been for retired nurses of both sexes. He was a mere lad of eighty-nine, but he obviously reciprocated her feelings. They got engaged and there was even talk of marriage.

Nurse Jones was completely revitalised. Alas she was perhaps over-vitalised. The excitement proved too much for her and she had a stroke. As soon as she was over the worst of it and could manage a wheelchair, Nurse Jones travelled round to see every patient in the nursing home, including her fiancé, to say goodbye to them. She didn't miss a single person and it was quite a physical effort to push herself round the whole place. Having said goodbye to everybody, she got into her bed and from then on refused any food, drink or medication and died within forty-eight hours.

The lives of the two old ladies, Auntie Kitty and Nurse Jones were almost opposites. Auntie Kitty was sustained for four score years by a love that was extinguished too soon. Nurse Jones was struck down by a sudden burst of love at the age of ninety-five which proved too much for her. But both were remarkable and unique old ladies.

*   *   *

Unfortunately not all my patients reached the great ages of Auntie Kitty and Nurse Jones. Death sometimes came like an epidemic and one seemed to be dealing more with death than life. It is a situation in any circumstance I have always found extremely difficult to deal with. I have never been able to detach myself from the emotions of the bereaved. I have always felt that I wanted to weep with them. And when it was people that I knew well, and particularly people that I worked with, it became almost too much to bear.

I had worked with Amazing Grace, our much beloved receptionist, for more than twelve years. She was always a source of laughter and warmth and reassurance, and the patients loved her. During the twelve years I knew her she had to bear the ordeal of losing two husbands, both war heroes who had lost limbs, and who both died of a cancer of the stomach. Somehow she survived these awful losses and kept going. Then Grace herself was taken ill and although she struggled on to work almost to the bitter end, in six short months she changed from a laughing, outgoing person, to one whose total energies were absorbed in fighting off pain.

She never lost her sense of humour. In hospital the day before she died, she winked at me, pointed across at the woman in the next bed, and said, 'She's a silly old bugger.' This was typically Grace, joking through the most awful pain.

There was a massive turnout for her funeral and a strange sort of quiet has remained in the surgery waiting room ever since. She was always prepared to listen to our troubles. She would always cheer us up. She always decorated the surgery at Christmas. She always put up the Christmas tree. She was a very special person and her loss shattered us all.

We bought a special armchair with a little plaque engraved in her memory which is kept in the waiting room for the more disabled patients. By doing that, we felt that part of Grace would always remain with us.

The same week that Grace died Jackie Dean, a woman doctor colleague I had visited every week for fifteen years, also – mercifully – died. Jackie had innumerable conditions which had kept her virtually bedridden for about ten years. Her only trips from her bedroom were down an electric chair-lift. She was nursed by her devoted sister who somehow had kept her clear of bed sores. Always fresh and pink, Jackie would try and have her hair done the day before I did my weekly call. She never complained about her medical condition and she had a myriad of conditions; a collapsed spine, a fractured arm that hadn't healed, a malabsorption syndrome, a broken leg.

I had sent her to London to my teaching hospital to see whether they could offer her anything. Having given her the fullest scrutiny, they said there was no treatment they could possibly offer her and they thought that at the outside she could only manage to survive about another two years.

This news was broken to the family but, mainly through the support and care of her sister Marie, she managed to have ten fulfilled years; fulfilled in that lots of people came to see her, she was always interested in what was going on, she could watch the TV at the end of the bed. We always had a joke when I went in to see her. Sometimes she would be wearing a riding hat; she had been a great rider in the past. She used to bet in mythical millions of pounds for me on televised horse races.

It was only in her latter months that things became miserable, when her condition had really deteriorated. She could understand what I said to her but we couldn't understand what she was saying to us. It was like a man on the stage answering questions into a microphone on which the wires had been cut.

Grace and Jackie died in the same week and their funerals were in the same week. Grace's was an Anglican funeral and Jackie's a Roman Catholic funeral where the family asked me to be among those who sprinkled holy water on her grave.

In this very same week, I was invited to be a guest in London at a Jewish dinner, a charity dinner for a home for elderly Jewish people. It was a tremendous experience. The top British Jewish families were there and the entrance to the dining place was swarming with security men with walkie-talkies. There was a magnificent dinner. Three or four hun-

114

dred people were there and pledge cards were placed in front of all the diners except for my host and me, as my host had made some large donation from a trust fund and was exempt from pledging. To my utter amazement it was announced at the end of the dinner that the amount of money pledged from the assembled company was more than a million pounds. This million pounds was to be used for the succour of their elderly dependents.

At the end of the dinner a grace was sung which was very similar to one of the addresses given by the Roman Catholic priest at Jackie Dean's funeral and both were in many ways similar to parts of the service for Grace. Exposed to three different branches of religion in the same week I was struck by their sameness.

When I pick up my daily newspaper and see the various conflicts raging round the world, the Middle East, Northern Ireland, Iran, the vast majority of them seem to be over some religious difference. What a great pity that mankind has not yet learnt to concentrate on the things that we have in common rather that fight over the things we differ about.

CHAPTER 13

Medical Advances

Henry Cooper was a mechanic at the Tadchester Garage; a wiry young man in his early twenties. His famous name, alas, brought him no favours, just liabilities. Hardly a day passed without somebody splashing him with Brut or shouting 'Give us your left hook, Henry!'

The witticisms he had to put up with were about as original as those of one of the nurse's husbands who, at each hospital Christmas party, would say inevitably, 'Is there a doctor in the house?' as if he were making a highly original joke.

Being the centre of attention upset Henry to the extent that he became quite withdrawn and mixed very little with his mates, spending all his time either fiddling with cars at home or going out with his fiancée, Alice who worked in the garage office. He was a most obliging and pleasant young man. If I got a puncture or a mechanical breakdown out of hours I knew I could always call for Henry and he would nip along and fix it.

I am sure his parents never knew the handicap that they were putting on him when they called him Henry. It was an even greater handicap than that of another patient called Down, whose parents christened her Ida, thus making sure that at least her school life was hell on earth.

Henry came to the surgery one day. He had been on holiday in Cornwall and had had to go to a doctor with a swelling on his neck. The doctor said it was a strained muscle, but when I saw him he had a large round swelling in his neck which was obviously not a muscle. I sent him off to see a specialist in Winchcombe and a diagnosis of Hodgkin's disease was made.

Hodgkin's is a disease of the lymph glands, and it brought back horrific memories of one of the first clinical cases I saw as a medical student. In outpatients was a most beautiful Swedish girl in her early twenties, and the consultant made us all go and feel some glands in her neck. This particular consultant was an unpleasant and tactless pontificator and, having asked us all what we thought it might be, he asked what was going to happen to the girl. We all put our various ideas forward and then, almost in triumph he said, 'Whatever treatment we give her she will be dead within two years at the most.'

This shattered me completely. I just could not believe that such an awful thing could happen. In those days there was no treatment for this condition. It was my first brush with the awful realities of life. That night I explored my own body and my hair stood on end when I found a large gland under my left arm.

For months I haunted my student friends, getting them to feel the gland. I was positive I had the same condition as this girl. I took out a life insurance policy that didn't require a medical to provide some benefit for my family and cover any debts I might have. I remember sitting down for a dinner at Christmas and looking round at the family thinking that this was probably going to be my last Christmas on earth.

I continued like this until one day after a rugby match. We had just beaten Coventry at home on the morning of an international, a great triumph for the hospital, and all the players were celebrating after the game, while I was sitting morosely fingering my gland. Taffy Williams, the fly half, came up to me without any warning and gave me a terrific kick on the behind.

He said, 'I've been wanting to do that for the last few months. Stop fingering that stupid gland. We've all got glands.'

And of course we have. If any of us examine ourselves we've got glands in our necks, under our arms and in our groins; it's quite normal for us to have them. Taffy's kick worked. As one of my colleagues reminded me thirty years later I was one of the few people to get over Hodgkin's disease without having any treatment.

The situation for Henry was quite different from the poor Swedish girl. Hodgkin's disease is now quite curable. It may mean a fairly prolonged course of treatment but I am able to tell patients that they are going to get better. The treatment would probably be a mixture of radiotherapy – that's X-rays – and chemotherapy, drugs.

Henry went off and had his treatment. He lost his hair for a time but it all grew again. He came back to work fit and well. He got married and actually did live happily ever after. I so wished that this treatment had been available for the beautiful girl of my student days.

It sometimes happens, when you see one particular type of case, that you get a whole run of similar cases. Then you may go many years or even forever, without seeing anything similar. Henry was the first case of Hodgkin's disease that I had seen since I had started in practice, but in the following six months I saw three similar conditions.

One was a free church minister who had suddenly become yellow. The reason that he had turned yellow was that he had developed a glandular disorder, not exactly the same as, but similar to, Henry's. He went off like Henry to the radiotherapy/chemotherapy clinic. He was cured, and after his treatment was promoted to one of the most senior positions in the church.

One of the sea captains coming into Tadchester also had a lump, again not quite the same as Henry's but similar. This was called a lymphoma. For this they had to try several treatments. At one stage, having almost given up, they tried one further drug which completely cured him. He made a complete recovery and went back to skippering his boat as if nothing had happened.

My last patient during this spell was our grocery delivery boy who had a swelling on his testicles which turned out to be malignant. He went off to the radiotherapy/chemotherapy department and they cured him too. The outlook for this particular condition now is excellent whereas twenty years ago it was very poor. Our grocery lad, like Henry, lost his hair during his treatment but it came back and I would see him riding his bike about, back at work, fit as a flea.

'No problems Jack?' I asked one day as he delivered our groceries from a basket in the front of an old-fashioned sit-up-and-beg bike.

'No, I'm fine, Doctor. They call me the Bob Champion of Tadchester nowadays.'

I think there was a distinct advantage in being called Bob Champion rather than Henry Cooper. Nobody squirted you with Brut.

I had played no part in the treatment of any of these four cases. They had all been treated by these new and thriving departments of radio and chemotherapy. It is likely that the management in the future of disease will lie much more along these lines and will rely less on surgery than it has done in the past.

When penicillin was discovered, five conditions that previously always had been fatal, became completely treatable. The equivalent progress is now being made in the radiotherapy/chemotherapy field. It means that there is rarely such a thing as a hopeless case, and a cure for a condition considered untreatable may be only days away from being discovered. There is no doubt that we are becoming increasingly expert at keeping people alive. What we do not know, of course, is what they will do with their lives.

I remember the Roald Dahl story of the obstetrician who, using all his skill, managed to deliver a live baby where perhaps nine out of ten other consultants would have failed. When all was tidied up, the consultant went to the mother and said, 'What are you going to call the baby?'

The beaming mother looked up and said, 'Adolf.'

'That's a fine name, Mrs Hitler,' said the obstetrician.

CHAPTER 14

Creatures Small and Small

My patients on the whole were a self-respecting lot, and even the poorest kept their little homes spick and span. There were a few exceptions, though, whose houses had never known the flick of a duster or the hum of a vacuum cleaner for years. I'd be called out to a home confinement now and again, and come back wondering how a baby could possibly survive among all the filth.

If I had time after such a call, my first job was to rush home, have a shower and a complete change of clothes in case I'd picked up any little strangers during my visit. Yes – fleas.

I'd read the occasional magazine article on the decline of the flea circus, complete with quotes from sideshow entrepreneurs bemoaning the fact that human fleas these days are almost impossible to come by. I could have given them a few addresses in Tadchester which would keep a dozen flea circuses fully staffed for twelve months of the year.

One tip I was given by an old country practitioner was to sprinkle flea powder into my trouser turn-ups before I called at a house known to harbour vermin. That took care of the dozier fleas who alighted on my trouser bottoms after a half-hearted hop from the carpet, but it could have no effect on the more energetic ones who leapt higher.

Often I'd be convinced I was hopping with fleas, when actually there wouldn't be a single one on me, but I reckon I'm entitled to get paranoid about things like that: patients would soon lose respect for a doctor who sat there scratching and swatting while they told him their symptoms.

The paranoia goes back some years, to when Jane was about four. I'd been on a visit to a particularly unsavoury house, and couldn't wait to get home and change. Unfortunately, my evening surgery was late, we had people coming to dinner, and I didn't have time to do more than have a wash and change my shirt.

I was about to come down and give a belated welcome to our guests when I felt a tickle on my chest. A flea? In my vest? Of all the times ...

'Quick, Pam,' I said, taking off my shirt and vest. 'I'm sure I've picked up fleas at that house! Have a quick look, would you?'

Pam inspected me, pronounced me flea-free, but ran for a clean vest just in case.

I hadn't realised that Jane was sitting in a corner of the room, playing quietly with her doll. She left the bedroom after Pam, and wandered down into the lounge where Trevor was doing his best to entertain our friends on his trumpet.

'Daddy won't be long,' she announced. 'He'll be here as soon as Mummy's got rid of his fleas ...'

Fleas weren't the only embarrassing condition that cropped up in general practice. Happily we managed to keep clear of most of the others. In the Sixties and Seventies, a scourge of every level of society was scabies. In the past it had been confined to groups of the unwashed, people with bad hygiene and people who shared a higher number of bedmates than normal. Something changed in the nature of the spread of this disease; it became no respecter of person or class, however good their hygiene, and turned up everywhere.

Scabies is a little mite that burrows under the skin – the burrowing can be seen under a large magnifying glass – and causes intense irritation. The irritation is worse when one is warm in bed at night and the most refined people used to appear in the surgery. One titled family, in which the grandfather, parents, children and grandchildren, including an eight-month-old baby, were all afflicted by this condition and came into the surgery looking as if they were all suffering from St Vitus' dance. My suggestion that they should all give each other wire brushes for Christmas wasn't well received.

The trouble with scabies is that it imitates many other skin conditions and is very similar to an allergy. However, the treatment, once the condition is proved, is very simple. It means having a hot bath, scrubbing yourself all over with a soft nailbrush and then being painted from head to foot with a liquid, keeping this liquid on for twenty-four hours. Follow this with a bath, a change of clean clothes and bed linen, and it's all over. In fact this is often the way in which the diagnosis is proved: if this treatment clears the widespread itchy skin condition, then you have had scabies. It's sometimes worth doing purely as a diagnostic measure, though it's not always a condition that people accept too well.

Other embarrassing conditions are worms, which most of us have had at some time. There are a great variety. Patients bring these rare delicacies to the surgery, wrapped in newspaper or in little jars, horrified that they may have a terminal illness. But, like scabies, most worms are easily eradicated. This is not so of a tapeworm which does take a real bit of shifting, but fortunately these are very rarely seen. I have only seen one in my whole medical life.

One of the most widespread of the embarrassing conditions is dysentry. The expression, 'It only hurts when I laugh,' is only topped by, 'You just don't know what happens when I sneeze'. Dysentry, like scabies and fleas, is no respecter of persons. With increased foreign travel, with people arriving from more and more different parts of the earth, not only do we get increases in outbursts of this condition, but we get an increase in variety. It's amazing how it can spread through close communities.

I had a friend whose misfortune was to be the medical officer to a leading British prep school. This prep school, whose pupils were children of really wealthy people, provided boys for the top public schools when they reached the magic age of thirteen. Among them would be some of the nation's future leaders: cabinet ministers, even prime ministers.

The school was struck by a particularly vicious dysentry bug that just wouldn't go away. It started with just one or two boys, then eventually the whole school was overwhelmed. This meant that stool specimens had to be obtained from every single boy in the school, every single person in the kitchens, all the indoor staff and all the outdoor staff. This was a major feat on its own. But when every possible suspect stool had been collected and examined the epidemic still didn't abate. The cook, who wasn't responsible but whom everyone thought might be, almost committed suicide. Then, because the epidemic showed no sign of dying down, investigations had to be made further afield.

After specimens from everybody in the school and its entourage had been examined, specimens from each member of the boys' families had to be obtained. There was the spectacle for a few days of streams of Rolls-Royces purring to a halt outside the school with embarrassed chauffeurs bringing in collections of little pots, perhaps feeling that their contracts of employment did not cover this end of the business.

In spite of these massive investigations, the condition still would not go away. Some mothers thought it was an Act of God. The school was persuaded to hold prayer meetings and a repressed mass hysteria set in.

Eventually the school was shut for half a term. When it reopened for the following term there was, thankfully, no sign of the disease. Its effects weren't entirely negative, however; many members of the upper crust had gained a wider experience of the fundamentals of life that might help to widen their understanding in the future.

One other, fairly recent, social leveller is ringworm. Children from the pony clubs and even people from the hunts came in with small patches of eczema to be cleared up. They were horrified to learn that they had contracted ringworm, almost certainly from their precious quadrupeds.

Once having got ringworm, it's very easy, like scabies to pass it round the family. It can be very stubborn and difficult to get rid of.

The most unfortunate member of the horsey set was a beautiful young lady in her early twenties who, the night before a special hunt ball, came to me desperately in need of help. She not only had ringworm, but scabies and dysentry as well. A holiday in Greece a few weeks before could easily have accounted for the additional problems. I had to tell her reluctantly that however much she was itching to, not to go to the ball. Not only would she be in danger of infecting fellow guests, she might even infect a few horses and I am sure the chauffeurs' union, or whoever represents these long-suffering gentlemen, would have objected to their queuing up with specimens from those large family pets, for inspection.

I was medical officer to Drake's College, a middle-ranking public school. It had a good, solid reputation and the boys came literally from all four corners of the earth.

We had our share of embarrassing parasites but ours had a touch of class about them. Boys with worms usually had them of the more exotic type, such as a Nigerian spearhead or bilharzia from the Middle East. We even had cases of malaria and once a case of typhoid. Specimens sent to the path lab from boys returning from outlandish places always caused a certain degree of excitement. Boys had worms, like most other people, but very rarely fleas. There was the odd case of dhobi's itch, which is a sort of athlete's foot of the groin. Altogether, we were rather proud of our overseas infestations; they gave us a slight edge over the local *hoi polloi*.

That is until one day when Matron came to me with a very long face.

'Doctor Bob,' she said, 'I'm afraid we have trouble.'

My thoughts immediately ran to diphtheria, meningitis, polio.

'What now?' I said, bracing myself for the worst.

'I'm afraid the whole school is down with nits.'

Unfortunately the news leaked out to the local grammar school. The pupils there, all being day boys, tended not to suffer from community diseases.

Nits, or head lice, once they get a hold in the school, take a great deal of shifting. It meant that whole forms of boys at a time had to have head inspections and special shampoos and lotions. The school never quite lived it down, and in clashes between local youths and boys at Drake's College the Drake's College boys were always referred to as 'nitwits'.

Taking the longer view, worms, fleas and nits are all part of growing up. However fastidious you are about your cleanliness and general hygiene you are lucky to pass through childhood and adolescence without at some time having at least one, if not all three.

126

A postcard dealing with the subject of worms was the second dirty story that I ever told, at a large family gathering. I was about four-and-a-half and could read. I had seen, on a postcard at the seaside a lady, looking down at a boy fishing in a river. The woman said to the little boy, 'Do you find it difficult fishing with worms young man?'

'No,' replied the boy. 'I've had them since I was three.'

This did not provoke quite the same hostile reaction that my first dirty story did, told at the age of three also to a large family gathering, when 'The same to you with knobs on' was the phrase of the moment.

'I have a story to tell,' I said.

'Yes Bobby,' said all the relatives, looking at this little golden-haired angel. 'What is it?'

'Well,' I said, 'Mae West went up to Primo Carnera and patted his chest and said "What a fine chest you've got"'.

'Yes Bobby,' said all the admiring relatives. 'And what did Carnera say to Mae West?'

'The same to you with knobs on,' said I, smiling in triumph.

It took me some years to understand why my uncle, who was sitting next to me, gave me a good clip round the ear and sent me straight up to bed.

* * *

Many people, have phobias about small creatures. At the top of the phobia list is spiders. And at the top of the spider phobia list was our slim, long-legged secretary-typist, Jean.

She said that the bravest thing that she ever did in her life was once when her husband was away and she found a spider in the bath. She nearly ran out of the house, but she plucked up courage, got the spider on a piece of paper, put one of her best teacups over the paper and flung both teacup and paper and spider out of the window. Unfortunately, this meant that from then on she could only have five people sitting down for tea at the same time.

Jean had inherited this phobia from her mother. Once, on holiday in Guernsey, with some sort of kamikaze instinct, they decided to visit a butterfly farm. They walked into a beautiful greenhouse with soft music playing in the background, beautiful flowers, fountains, peace and quiet. Walking towards them was a man with something on his hand. Jean's mother took a quick look. It was in fact a butterfly but, from where she looked she thought it was a spider. She screamed at the top of her voice, grabbing hold of Jean in one of her softer, tenderer parts which, for example, she wouldn't have been able to grab on Jean's brother Robert.

Her screams set loose a swarm which filled the whole of the huge greenhouse with a madly fluttering cloud. Mother and daughter, with eyes shut, had to be led out and revived with brandy. There was even talk of admitting them to hospital, but

128

it was wonderful what fresh air and a couple of tots of brandy did for them. What was unfortunate was that Jean's husband had already bought a memento of the holiday – a butterfly brooch.

CHAPTER 15

Different Ways

There was an upsurge in physical activity in Tadchester. There were more cricket teams, more football teams, athletic teams, swimming teams, rowing teams than there had ever been before. I think it reflected partly on the state of the economy. Some of the unemployed swelled the ranks of the various teams, of course, but what was more significant was that a lot of men were taking early retirement in their mid-fifties and early sixties. Any club is only as good as the committee running it. Now there were available a lot of middle-aged men, past their own days of active sport, willing to give a hand in running clubs.

It was most encouraging. Half the cricketers played Saturdays and Sundays for two different teams and, the vast majority of footballers played Saturday afternoon and Sunday morning.

Tadchester still boasted two semi-professional teams. One, Tadchester United, played from the council stadium as usual importing all its players except the odd one. The other team, Tadchester Royals, played in a much superior sort of stadium Up-the-Hill. The rugby club, who used to share the council ground, had now built a ground of their own with first class changing facilities, club house and bar, and flourished.

For the second time in the town's history one of the football clubs, Tadchester Royals, reached the first round of the F.A. Cup proper and played a third division side at home. However, they only managed to draw and lost the away fixture but there was great excitement in the town on the day of the cup tie.

The rugby club grew stronger and got better fixtures. They even entertained Cardiff Rugby Club on tour and gave them a very good game. The town, not very sports-minded before now, had two flourishing athletic clubs.

A girl came to see me in the surgery one night who was so thin I thought she must have anorexia nervosa, the slimmers' disease. She was in fact a champion three-thousand-metre runner on the verge of an international career and had pulled a muscle in her calf. Her calf seemed to be all sinew and bone; there was hardly room for muscle. Happily she soon responded to my treatment.

The best cricket club by far was Stowin, who often included in their Sunday games members of the Somerset county side. Sanford-on-Sea would strongly dispute this fact and games between the two clubs were battles royal. Sanford-on-Sea would raise their game to the height of their better opponents and usually came away with credit, if not as victors.

Regatta week was exciting. The number of crews competing gradually increased each year, but the fair that came for the week of the Regatta changed much in nature. The boxing booth went, there were no tents showing three-headed lambs, tattooed ladies or shows offering glimpses of partly clad ladies. These side shows were replaced by terrifying new types of roundabouts, whirligigs, rollercoasters that almost seemed to have entered the space age. It amazed me that they didn't take off and fly out to sea. Most people seemed to thoroughly enjoy them. I know all of them would have made me sick.

The carnival which in years gone by had been the highlight of the year, still tottered on. It was about half what it used to be but, it was still quite a creditable performance. Much of the trouble was that there were, as opposed to the number of people willing to help organise sporting activities, few people were prepared to give up their time for the carnival. Part of the reason for this was the fact that the carnival, in the past, had been a great help in financing Tadchester Hospital, the town's own hospital that belonged to the community. Now it belonged to the government. Although there were worthy causes like the new Cheshire Home and the new Hospice and they were raising money at Winchcombe for a body scanner, it wasn't quite the same.

This year there were a few more floats than usual and a lot of hard work had been put into them. The carnival queen looked gorgeous and was surrounded by pretty girls and boys all

dressed up in their finery with their proud parents watching. It was a fine day and it looked grand as it came round the corner for its main procession along the quay where most of the spectators were gathered.

It was at this point that things started to go wrong and probably made it the last carnival that Tadchester would hold. A few drunken youths started to pelt the floats with eggs, fruit and vegetables.

The Tadchester rugby club, who were all dressed as pirates and were doing the collecting, took immediate and vicious revenge on the hooligans and terrible fighting broke out all the way along the quay. Young children jumped terrified from the floats, looking for their parents. There were pirates and a few parents locked in fierce battle with the drunken louts. The rugby club made thirty-four citizens' arrests, three of the people arrested finishing up with broken arms. It brought the whole carnival to a halt. Gradually parents claimed their children or some neighbour took them away, and the beautiful float lorries that so much time had been spent on, went back home in tatters. Meanwhile, the snarling rugby pirates, backed by dozens of spectators, herded the bunch of arrested youths towards the police station.

There were only about half a dozen policemen on duty altogether, and they were quite beyond coping with all the melée down on the quay. It was all a terrible shame. There was a special court hearing. All those arrested were put on bail and, when their hearing came up, were fined £25 each and bound over to keep the peace. The ones with broken arms said they were going to sue the rugby club. Many of the parents said they were going to take private summonses out against the louts for damage to material and property, but of course nobody ever did.

On the night of the fracas, a few dozen leather-jacketed motorcyclists came over from Winchcombe and joined up with the remnants of the louts who had escaped being caught in the afternoon's activities. They must have been about sixty or seventy strong. They filled themselves up with beer, formed up in a column and marched towards the fairground singing, 'We stopped the carnival! We stopped the carnival'.

The fairground people seemed perfectly capable of dealing with the situation. As the mob got closer, getting braver as they sang, suddenly all the way along the footpath of the fairground appeared men in sweatshirts and overalls, each holding a huge monkey wrench or a piece of lead piping, saying nothing, doing nothing, just watching. The marching singers could see clearly that it would mean a broken skull rather than a broken arm if they came anywhere near this lot. Their singing gradually faltered as they walked past the fairground.

People attending the fair began to boo them, remembering the afternoon's chaos. A threatening crowd began to gather, the leather-jacketed toughs sobered up very quickly. A police car whizzed up and the local inspector got out and cooled the whole situation. He marched the motorcyclists and local boys, visibly displaying a truncheon in his hand, back to where their motorbikes were, saw them on their bikes then made the local youths queue up while a police constable took the names of each one.

Such incidents are sad reflections on our time. In Tadchester we're lucky: we suffer less from this sort of thing than most places. As yet nobody has found a proper answer ...

* * *

The health of Tadchester, like everywhere else, appeared to improve. People seemed to be living longer, the general health was good, and we got fewer night calls. I think this was mainly because we had better drugs.

One of the common night calls in the old days was for a condition called paroxysmal nocturnal dyspnoea, or cardiac asthma: in simple terms, some people suddenly had attacks of breathlessness at night. It meant that when they went to bed, the left side of their heart came under some strain. Now better drugs, particularly ones that make the body lose surplus water, have virtually eliminated this condition as a night call. And people who had good nights generally had better days.

However, there was one change in the world of medicine, doctors were no longer the only people to turn to when you became ill.

Tadchester, like most of the country was going through a time when alternative medicines of one sort or another were the vogue. All alternative medicines enjoy one of the same benefits that conventional medicine has: namely that the vast majority of people get better without any attention, and sometimes in spite of the attention they are receiving. When they are getting better, they tend to give credit either to the medicine they are taking or the person who is looking after them, whereas the healer is actually good old Mother Nature.

Some patients' attitudes changed. A patient you had known well, who had perhaps been attending for years, would come and say sneeringly, 'Thank goodness I've stopped taking the muck that you've been giving me all these years.' He would then outline his present treatment, which could be anything from carrot juice to yoga which had completely revitalised him, helped him to discover his inner self and completely stabilised him. The fact that usually, after a few months, at least ninety-five per cent of such patients were back with the same old problems, didn't seem to lessen their contempt for conventional medicine.

I was summoned to the bedside of one lady patient who was, as she said, in a complete state of exhaustion. Admittedly she had had a few games of tennis that morning and was hoping to go to a ball the following night. Apart from answering a few questions, she conducted the whole conversation as a monologue for an hour and a half. She had at last found the answer to her problems. She almost despised the medical profession; we just didn't understand things. Although she was completely exhausted she was going to seek no help from us any more and, by the way, would it be all right if she went up to London to a wedding on the Saturday?

I had to learn to take such things in my stride. This particular lady was back again in a month's time repeating that nobody in the medical profession understood her problems which had all come back again. I hadn't the heart to remind her that only four weeks earlier she had cured herself.

This lady personally explored several branches of medicine. On each occasion she came back triumphantly to say that her condition was not nervous, that some unqualified doctor had found that vitamin lack or hormone imbalance was her trouble. She refused to accept the fact that the source of her whole trouble was perhaps a basic depression which would have responded to the right drugs prescribed by a qualified psychiatrist. To accept her depression would have meant losing face with herself, and when she did see the psychiatrist she said he was a rude man who just didn't understand her complaint. There is no answer to this sort of patient. You have to accept that some patients will always be like this, and that you can't be all things to all men. Or women, either.

*   *   *

When I was a medical student I met, on a television programme, a taxi driver/writer/philosopher called Herbert Hodge. He became a great friend.

Herbert, one of the most honest men I have ever met, was ahead of his time. Among many other literary achievements, he wrote a weekly philosophical article in *John Bull* magazine. I always remember two things that he said to me. Once, after dealing with a particularly depressing bout of patients, I had thought of emigrating to Canada. Herbert wrote me a long letter saying that I should remember that, wherever I went, I would only be taking myself with me.

I think this was a major factor in my not uprooting the family and going to Canada. Going abroad would not make me a different person, and I would find the same problems that I was having to deal with now. And it certainly wouldn't be any easier three thousand miles away from familiar surroundings.

His other suggestion was that society should provide professional listeners. I think he had a point. They would be people whom you could go to and unashamedly pour out all your woes. The professional listener, having accepted his fee,

would have to listen, not necessarily make any comment but to give people an opportunity to get things off their chests.

Many of the branches of alternative medicine are very close to filling the suggestion that Herbert made twenty years ago. There are growing numbers of counsellors, often having links with psychiatrists or general practices. Many of them, alas, cannot be included in the scheme of the National Health Service but for £35 an hour, you can pour out your woes to them. You can approach them directly without being referred by your doctor. The counsellors are often a tremendous help, doing that most precious of all things, saving peoples' faces with themselves.

Other alternative branches are better known, such as chiropractic, osteopathy and the fast-growing one of acupuncture. None of these are completely divorced from conventional medicine, and many doctors have become qualified in these additional skills. There was a general practice in Winchcombe where two of the partners were excellent manipulative surgeons and achieved marvellous results with patients we sent to them.

Non-medically qualified chiropractors, osteopaths and acupuncturists vary from the very good to the very bad. I have known patients who have greatly benefited from these alternative forms of medicine. Similarly, I have known others lose a great deal of money with no benefit. Others still, by seeking such help without being conventionally assessed, delayed the diagnosis of more serious medical problems.

I remember at least two cases of patients in great pain being manipulated by an unqualified or non-medically qualified osteopath. They were discovered to have cancerous growths in their spines, and had not had this possibility excluded before the treatment.

Another change in medicine is the increasing availability of medicine under private schemes. This has a balance of good and bad. It means people can skip National Health hospital waiting lists for medical treatment. This sounds unfair, but it does make National Health waiting lists shorter and if a man has a one-man business he can't afford not to be there.

I accept that people have a right, if they want to, to spend money on their body. What is most irritating, and this really the fault of my consultant colleagues as opposed to the patients, is when my own patients announce that they have just changed their gynaecologist, or their new psychiatrist has put them on a new form of medication.

The consultants are breaking medical ethical rules in that they should only see patients who have been referred by general practitioners. Not that general practitioners are infallible, but there is a loss of continuity of care of patients; neither the general practitioner nor the consultant knows what the other is giving the patient.

The whole situation may become self-limiting as my consultant colleagues' fees become more and more expensive. The time may come when the private medical schemes are likely to founder because the doctors and the independent nursing homes they run, have priced themselves out of the market.

However, in spite of this recent growth of alternative medicine and private medicine, it made no difference to our medical load at Tadchester, which seemed to steadily increase year by year.

Two new areas of medical care that sprang up locally were of tremendous benefit to the community and I couldn't speak too highly of both organisations. One was a hospice at Stowin, which Steve Maxwell was very much involved with. He was concerned mainly with the care of the dying and terminally ill, but people with long illnesses also used to go there for periods of rest and recuperation and to give their families a break from looking after them.

Strangely, the hospices were happy places. Patients were well looked after, the staff were experts at keeping people free from pain, and patients were allowed to die with dignity in pleasant surroundings. What an advance from the days when there used to be hospitals with bold lettering on the gate announcing that this was St John's Hospital for the Dying.

Hospices seem to have found the right approach and to have attracted the right people to run them. They are beginning to solve the management of that most complicated aspect of life – namely, death.

A Cheshire Home opened halfway between Peargate and Sanford-on-Sea. It had good views of the sea and the bay and cared for the long-term ill and disabled.

Again, it attracted selfless people with the highest motivation to look after their less fortunate fellow men.

These two new establishments had a great influence over the whole of our area, and in general brought out the best in people. In fact it brought the best out of the whole community as fêtes, jumble sales and all kinds of fund-raising events were run to provide funds for both these places. It gave a sense of purpose and somehow I feel if they had been there before poor Tom Leatherbridge had been run out of St Peter's, he would probably have still been in Tadchester. But again that could well have been a mistake. His parish up north was the ideal place for him.

We used to make it a point that all five partners would meet for coffee every morning at eleven, and on the days Catherine worked she would join us as well. We then used to hand over cases of people we may have seen for a partner the night before or over the weekend. We also chatted generally about our problems. It was a great help to get things off one's chest, to talk about our worries and have our partners pat us on the back and say, 'Never mind, everything's going to be all right.'

I was always called on to give a thought for the day which usually meant telling a dirty story. With the coming of these many types of alternative medicine, I suggested that we knock nails upwards through the seats of the surgery chairs so that

patients could have instant acupuncture while they waited to see us. I also thought it might markedly cut down on the number of patients, as I am quite sure that a great number came just to snuggle in a comfortable chair in the warm. However, none of my partners would back me up, so we went on practising conventional western medicine as before.

CHAPTER 16

Going Home

Great changes were taking place in the surgery and in medical life in general. Soon after Grace's death, Gladys – our senior receptionist since long before I had arrived in the practice and who had been threatening to retire for many years – did retire. She was replaced by Denise in the new post of practice manager, Denise was a young, energetic, meticulous organiser.

Our longest serving employee was the faithful Avise who was head of dispensing, a great athlete even though she had a daughter at university, old enough to be on the fringe of the English athletic team. I would come into the surgery on a Monday morning, having spent the weekend huddled round the fire, to find that Avise had done a couple of half-marathons in the mud and sleet. To help her in the dispensary we had the vivacious dark-haired Sue who was spending part of her time at college training to be a qualified dispenser. After Grace's death we also had Sue's daughter Mandy helping us out for a year before she went off to become a medical student.

On the secretarial and typing side we had the calm, groomed, poised Victoria who acted as practice manager when Denise was away. There was also the hard-working Jean, the good-natured Ann who did two or three sessions in reception, and the conscientious Pat who probably had the longest association with the practice. Whenever Pat was on, there was always a cup of coffee waiting as soon as I arrived at my desk. Not least we had our treasure, Mrs Vincent, who kept us supplied with immaculate white coats, and with the help of her daughter, kept the surgery spick and span.

We had built an extra room to the surgery which enabled us to have two nurses, Deborah and Gill, who gradually increased the scope of their work so that they were now taking all the blood samples, ear syringing, dressing, treating varicose ulcers, doing some stitching themselves and running a Well Woman clinic. They had a blood pressure clinic, and their own immunisation clinic. Debbie and Gill also operated an electro-cardiogram which could be taken to patients' houses as well as being used in the surgery.

The final member of our indoor team, was our midwife, Amanda, a kind, caring, excellent midwife, successor to the stalwart Nurse Plank. Amanda was petite but made up in energy for anything she lacked in size. She was employed by the local health authority as opposed to being employed by us.

We were gradually building up into an expanding team offering fuller facilities. Where our work was decreasing was at the hospital. It was now almost completely transformed into a geriatric hospital with a few general practice beds and a casualty department. Henry Johnson could no longer do his surgical sessions there, and Jack Hart and I were no longer called on to do any anaesthetics. Ron Dickinson still took tonsils out but he had to go over to Winchcombe where a new main hospital had been built.

When I had first come to the practice we did virtually everything for our patients. I anaesthetised all my own emergencies as well as doing routine lists. All the midwifery was done at home or in the tiny nursing home in the town. We were virtually a self-contained unit. Now we worked in quite a different capacity.

Coming back from holiday, I found that at last we had been computerised. In the dispensary there was a row of what

looked like television sets, rolls of paper, telephones and other machines. All prescriptions for people who were on long term medication had to be computerised. You had just to quote a number and the computer would say if the patient had had too many pills or what pills were due. It was all quite terrifying. Even the typewriter terrified me. There was nothing more startling than to go into the office to have a word with whoever was typing, and find the typewriter tapping away on its own from its memory bank.

We did more surgeries now and fewer visits, but we seemed busier than we did when we worked much longer hours. I think this was because we tried to work office hours. When I first came to the practice the evening surgery started at six and went on until it finished. Now the evening surgery started at four and if the building hadn't been cleared by half past six all the staff were beginning to get agitated.

All consultations were made by appointment and Saturday mornings were for emergencies only. This was reasonable: patients would quite happily make an appointment to see their dentist during the week, fitting their business arrangements around it, but were horrified that the doctor would not be available to syringe their ears on a Saturday morning. We slowly educated them to the fact that we, like them, quite liked weekends off. Whatever hours they worked during the week, it was very rarely that they were called out of bed and, at the most, their total number of working hours was probably about half of ours.

Things always go round in circles. This was proved by one of the Winchcombe practices, a large practice of eight doctors whose morning appointments system was becoming overwhelmed. They stopped morning appointments in favour of a free-for-all, and kept appointments just for the afternoons and evenings, which was the system they'd used years ago.

It had been much the way with small hospitals. As soon as one enlightened government department had managed to shut them all down, another had the brilliant idea of opening them all up again as community hospitals. There was even talk, as the Tadchester hospital was reduced down to its new structure, of enlarging it to include some operating beds. But all this was in the distant future and they all required that most inaccessible material, money.

One of the biggest upsets of all however (apart from Grace's death, which really shook the structure of the practice) was that Steve Maxwell, our senior partner, was talking of retiring, or at least cutting his work to the absolute minimum as well as getting married. He had been such a good doctor, such a marvellous senior partner, counsellor, friend, philosopher, and probably the best man I had met in my life. He had been in practice in Tadchester for forty years, and it was difficult to imagine work in the practice without him.

His forthcoming wedding had the town absolutely buzzing. Few people could have been given more wedding presents that Steve. He is the only man that I know to have been given twenty-two toasters as wedding presents.

'I know why you're retiring,' I said to Steve, going into his consulting room one day to find half one wall covered with piles of gifts. 'You want to open a shop.'

Steve, who had managed every other problem in medicine

and life without a qualm, found his present situation almost too much to handle.

'Just think of all the letters to write,' he said surveying the hundred or so presents piled against the wall, 'and these are only some of them.'

I don't know whether it was the strain of the forthcoming wedding, but Steve certainly didn't look as well as usual. We tried to entice him out for a bachelor night but he would have none of it.

'Good heavens,' he said. 'I'm far too old for all that sort of nonsense.'

I popped into his consulting room at the end of his last surgery before the wedding. I found him sitting at his desk with a misty look in his eyes.

'You OK, Steve?' I asked.

'Fine, thanks, Bob,' he replied. 'Just thinking.'

'No last-minute regrets?'

'Good heavens, no,' he said, smiling. 'I just wish I'd done it sooner.'

Without any doubt Steve was the best-loved man in our town. Not only for his kindness and his meticulous medicine: many an attractive and well-educated spinster had hung on hoping one day perhaps, just perhaps, she might be playing the part that Nancy Doone, Steve's fiancée, would be playing from now on.

The day of the wedding dawned. There was tremendous excitement in Tadchester. It was almost like a carnival day. The whole town turned out to see them married at St Mary's Church and those who couldn't get into the church lined the streets and cheered them as if they were royalty. The sun shone magnificently. All traces of whatever strain I saw in Steve's face had gone, and on his wedding day both he and the bride looked happy and radiant.

There was no formal reception. The wedding party moved to the town hall where there were drinks and toasts before they got into Steve's car and drove away. The crowd had patiently waited outside and there were more crowds of people waving and cheering right up until the outskirts of the town.

Steve was sixty-seven when he married. It was so good to see him so happy and with the perfect bride. I hoped that many years of happiness lay ahead of him.

*   *   *

The wedding had an extra bonus for us in that all the children had come home for it. Paul and Gill came from Aldermaston with the news that Gill might be making us grandparents in six or seven months' time. Trevor and Jane travelled up from Brighton.

Jane had passed her degree in the history of design and could not tear herself away from Brighton. She had worked both in the theatre workshop and in the Brighton Festival and in the main Brighton theatre, sometimes as a dresser. They had offered her a part-time permanent job there which fitted in well with her ambitions.

Jane wanted to make and design clothes. She had thought originally of opening a shop, but decided she would use the markets first. We had to provide her with sewing machines and overlockers and press-studders and a host of other equipment. The name of her shop, if it had have come off, would have been *Duff* and she made this the motif on her clothes labels. It was a mouth shouting 'Duff' and I personally thought it was awful – it looked like an advertisement for false teeth – but I am sure she was a much better judge of it than I was.

Trevor and Jane had found a large top-floor flat on the Brighton-Hove boundary with a view of the sea and beach and decided to buy it. It was half the price that Trevor would have had to pay in London and it did mean that they were between them investing in bricks and mortar.

It seemed strange for Pam and I to sit there and listen to

Paul and Gill talking about their house and bathroom fittings and to hear the most undomesticated person in the world, Trevor, coupled with one of the untidiest, Jane, talking about how spick and span they were keeping their flat. It was so lovely to have them all together – and Gill who had become just as important to us as any of our own children.

Eventually the time came for them to leave us. Both couples were setting off by car.

'Well,' said Jane, 'it's about time we were going home.'

'I'm afraid that goes for us, too,' said Paul.

We watched Paul and Gill get into their brand new firm's car and Jane and Trevor get into Trevor's Fiesta van and set off for home. This was the first time in our lives that where Pam and I had lived wasn't home for all our children. It almost cut us to the quick. Pam had tears in her eyes as she saw them go.

'Fancy, hearing them say that,' she said. 'That they're going home.'

'Well,' I said, 'we've two homes that we can always go and visit, and we've got a choice of Berkshire countryside and the Thames, or Brighton and the sea coast.'

'But the awful thing is that our home isn't their home any more,' said Pam. 'They have homes of their own.'

'Yes,' I replied. 'I'm afraid things are going to be different from now on.'

Postscript

There is the fable of the old man sitting outside a town, being approached by a stranger.

'What are they like in this town?' asked the stranger.

'What were they like in your last town?' replied the old man.

'They were delightful people. I was very happy there. They were kind, generous and would always help you in trouble.'

'You will find them very much like that in this town.'

The old man was approached by another stranger.

'What are the people like in this town?' asked the second stranger.

'What were they like in your last town?' replied the old man.

'It was an awful place. They were mean, unkind and nobody would ever help anybody.'

'I am afraid you will find it very much the same here,' said the old man.

* * *

If it should be your lot to ever visit Tadchester, this is how you will find us.

WHAT NEXT, DOCTOR?

Dr Robert Clifford

WHAT NEXT, DOCTOR? is the third book in the compelling saga of Dr Clifford's hilarious true-life experiences as a G.P. in a West Country practice.

Dr Clifford's chronicles commence when he and his bride wake up to a bizarre confrontation on the first day of their honeymoon – and promptly prescribe themselves champagne as a cure! The patients passing through his life are by turns comic and courageous, lovable and tragic. There's the long-married couple whose recipe for happiness is a row twice a week . . . the accident-prone ex-miner whose collection of injuries and ailments makes him a medical curiosity . . . and the elderly couple who turn out to be mother and son – the son is eighty-one!

Dr Clifford presents us with an immensely entertaining slice of life – the tragedies and triumphs of ordinary people caught up in the human drama of survival in a world of sickness and ill health. And he tells his tale with all the warmth and humour that make his books a real delight to read.

BIOGRAPHY/HUMOUR
0 7221 2381 7